Editor's Preface

Great economic and social changes have taken place in Europe in recent years. The agricultural workforce in the west was halved, for example, during the 1950s and 1960s. This unprecedented flight from the land has made possible some much-needed reorganization of farm holdings but it has also created problems, not least that of finding uses for land in the highlands and elsewhere where it is no longer profitable to farm. Closely related is the difficulty of maintaining services to a much diminished rural population or of providing new kinds of services for the holidaymakers who increasingly buy up rural properties.

Contraction of the labour force has also taken place in many traditional industries. The coal-mining industry alone has shed two-thirds of its workforce since 1950. The resulting problems have been especially serious in those mining or manufacturing districts which have a high level of dependence on a single source of employment—a not uncommon result of Europe's industrial past—and the efforts of those who seek to attract new industries are often thwarted by a legacy of pollution, bad housing, and soured labour relations.

Quite a different set of problems has arisen in the great cities of Europe such as London and Paris and in the conurbations of closely linked cities well exemplified by Randstad Holland. Here are problems due to growth brought about by the expansion of consumer-orientated manufacturing and still more by the massive increase in office jobs which proliferate in 'down-town' business districts. The problems are economic, social and political, and they include the effects of congestion, of soaring land values, of the increasing divorce of place of residence from place of work, and of the difficulty of planning a metropolitan region that may be shared between many independent-minded local authorities.

The problems resulting from change are not passing ones; indeed they exhibit a persistence that amply justifies their study on an areal basis. Hence the *Problem Regions of Europe* series. The volumes in the series have all been written by geographers who, by the nature of their discipline, can take a broadly based approach to description and analysis. Geographers in the past have been reluctant to base their studies on regions since the problem is of a temporary nature, less enduring than the 'personality' of the region but the concern with present-day problems has even resulted in the suggestion that regions should be defined in terms of the problems that confront them.

Certain themes emerge clearly when the basis of the problem is examined: the effects of a harsh environment, of remoteness and of political division, as well as of industrial decay or urban congestion. But these have not been examined in isolation and the studies that make up the series have been carefully chosen in order that useful comparisons can be made. Thus, for example, both the Mezzogiorno and Andalusia have to contend with the problems of Mediterranean drought, wind, and flood, but the precise nature of these and other problems, as well as man's response to them, differs in the two regions. Similarly, the response to economic change is not the same in North-East England as in North Rhine–Westphalia, nor the response to social pressures the same in Paris as in the Randstad.

The efforts which individual governments have made to grapple with their problems provides a basis for critical assessment in each of the volumes. For too long solutions were sought that were piecemeal and short-term. Our own Development Areas in Britain provide a good illustration of this kind of policy. Of late, however, European governments have shown an increasing awareness of the need to undertake planning on a regional basis. The success or otherwise of such regional policies is fully explored in the individual *Problem Region* volumes.

When it was first planned the *Problem Region* series was thought of as useful only to the sixth-form student of geography. As it has developed it has become clear that the authors—all specialists in the geography of the areas concerned—have contributed studies that will be useful, not only for sixth-form work, but as a basis for the more detailed investigations undertaken by advanced students, both of geography and of European studies in general.

D.I.S.

St. Edmund Hall, Oxford
August 1973

3

Contents

1 Introduction: Northern Ireland as a Problem Region

There can be few who would question the case for including Northern Ireland in a series entitled 'Problem Regions of Europe'. The events of the late 1960s and early 1970s are sufficient evidence for the existence of deep-rooted problems in that region.

One of the many unfortunate consequences flowing from these events is the impression that the problems of Northern Ireland are rooted exclusively in incomprehensible Irish sectarianism or are exclusively economic and that a massive programme of economic aid is the panacea. In fact neither of these viewpoints comprises an adequate explanation. There are serious economic problems in Northern Ireland, but they exacerbate rather than explain the political problems. The political crisis in turn has economic implications, particularly affecting questions of confidence and economic growth, but here too it must not be assumed that it is solely responsible for the economic troubles.

The economic problems of Northern Ireland are probably the easiest to understand. Basically the province is suffering from an aged economic structure which grew up in the first Industrial Revolution. Thus the contraction of world markets for naval and merchant shipping, well organized competition from overseas countries in shipbuilding, aircraft, and heavy engineering, a growing use of synthetic fibres, and the failure of new forms of economic activity to employ as many persons as the old have given Northern Ireland a chronically high level of unemployment, poverty, and migration. These, however, are familiar modern problems common to other peripheral regions of the United Kingdom such as South Wales and the North-East of England and they are duplicated in the coalfield areas of Belgium in the European Community and West Virginia in the United States.

The political problem, however, is of a nature less easily understood in the context of modern British or European politics. The basic political question is one of national identity. Within the political unit of Northern Ireland one-third of the population of 1·5 million do not perceive themselves as being British. Rather, their loyalties gravitate towards the neighbouring Irish Republic which views all of the six north-eastern counties as unredeemed parts of its national territory.

This is in sharp contrast to the rest of the United Kingdom where political cleavages and issues run largely along socio-economic lines. In Europe as a whole the period when such national minority questions comprised the dominant political issues lasted from about the early nineteenth century until the end of the Second World War. Since then questions of international ideology, defence, and economic and political union have tended to predominate. Only in limited areas of eastern and south-eastern Europe and, more openly, in South Tyrol, do similar minority problems assume local dominance. Moreover, the problem is made doubly anachronistic by the fact that the chief cultural characteristic of each of the two national groups is their religion, thus harking back to the politico-religious cleavages of sixteenth-century England and continental Europe.

While the political and economic difficulties of Northern Ireland have been frequently discussed and their interrelationships rarely understood, the regional problems *within* the six counties have been relatively neglected. This is rather ironic, because it is in the context of the regional problems that a close relationship between several aspects of the economic and political problems can be discussed. The eastern counties of Antrim and Down have comprised the economic core area of north-east Ireland since the Industrial Revolution. Consequently, in the Belfast area especially, this has bequeathed a serious backlog of aged and obsolescent houses and public services and amenities. There are also serious problems due to modern growth of economic activity and population, since most new industrial activity has located in and around the Belfast region. The political problems of the east are also rather complex. This is the region where the Protestant and pro-British population is in a decided majority, but there are Catholic and anti-Partition minorities in all the chief urban centres and above all in Belfast where strict spatial segregation has posed a chronic problem. By contrast, the western areas of Northern Ireland are characterized by rural dwelling, heavy dependence on agriculture, relatively few alternative economic opportunities and a much higher level of unemployment. These are also districts where the Catholic and anti-Partition population are frequently in a position

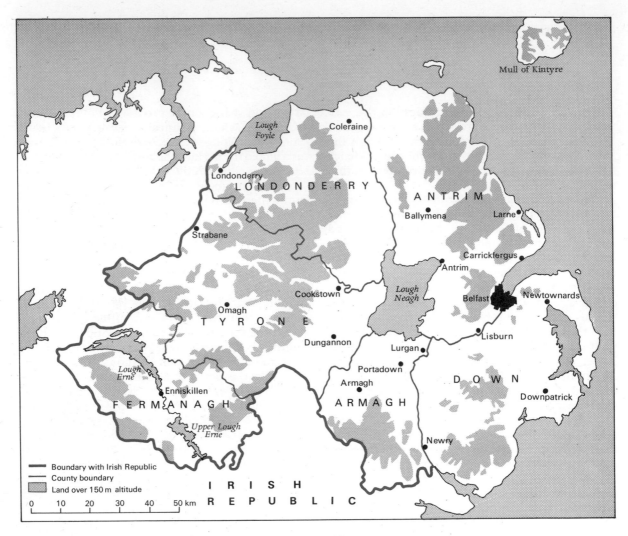

Fig. 1. Northern Ireland

of local numerical superiority. It was in such districts that the Protestants attempted to retain local control by such practices as manipulation of local authority boundaries and discriminatory allocation of housing and employment. It was in these fertile western areas that the earliest Civil Rights campaigns began in the late 1960s.

Thus Northern Ireland is presented as a problem region in several dimensions of time and space. The problems of economic readjustment are examined first, not because they are regarded as the most important, but because this is the aspect of the six counties' problem which places the region firmly in the mainstream of modern British and European affairs. The political problem is then discussed to show how in Northern Ireland the anachronistic question of national identity and sovereignty is not yet resolved. Finally, the regional problems demonstrate the duality of Northern Ireland and serve further to illustrate the complex relationship between the economic and the political problems.

2 The Economic Problem

The nature of the problem

Unemployment

Compared with the rest of the United Kingdom, Northern Ireland has a chronically high level of unemployment. Since 1945 it has fluctuated between 10 per cent and 6 per cent, and from 1965 onwards between 7·8 per cent and 6·1 per cent.

The overall level of unemployment in the United Kingdom since the mid-1960s has varied from 1·5 per cent (1965) to 2·7 per cent (1970). Generally speaking Northern Ireland has followed the general trend of economic activity in the rest of the country, but has differed in two important respects. First, any upward trend in the unemployment level of the United Kingdom as a whole is not only reproduced but exaggerated in the Northern Ireland economy. Thus when there was a rise of 1·0 per cent in United Kingdom unemployment between 1966 and 1967, the rise in Northern Ireland over the same period was 1·8 per cent. Secondly, the overall level of unemployment in Northern Ireland has persisted. Over the period 1965–70, the percentage unemployed has exceeded that in the rest of the United Kingdom by an average of 4·68 per cent.

The only regions of the United Kingdom with almost comparable unemployment levels are Wales, Scotland, and Northern England (Table 1). Here too the levels of unemployment have been consistently above the rest of the country since the mid-1960s, suggesting that Northern Ireland is merely sharing a characteristic common to peripheral regions of the United Kingdom. However, even at its worst in 1969 and 1970, the unemployed percentage in Northern England was always at least 2·2 per cent below the Northern Irish level.

There were certain encouraging trends during the late 1960s and early 1970s. Particularly notable was the fall from the high level of 7·8 per cent in 1967 to 7·0 per cent in 1970. This occurred at a time when the British economy was virtually stagnant, the overall national level of unemployment was static or rising slightly, and in spite of the political upheavals since 1968. However, even allowing for these qualifications, it remained a serious problem that the region persisted in having the highest level of unemployment in the United Kingdom, and a large section of its valuable human resources unused.

TABLE I

Percentage of total insured population registered as unemployed

	1965	1966	1967	1968	1969	1970
United Kingdom	1·5	1·6	2·5	2·5	2·5	2·7
Great Britain	1·4	1·5	2·4	2·4	2·4	2·6
England	1·2	1·3	2·2	2·2	2·2	2·4
North	2·6	2·6	4·0	4·7	4·8	4·8
Yorkshire and Humberside	1·1	1·2	2·1	2·6	2·6	2·9
East Midlands	0·9	1·1	1·8	1·9	2·0	2·3
East Anglia	1·3	1·4	2·1	2·0	1·9	2·1
South-East	0·9	1·0	1·7	1·6	1·6	1·7
South-West	1·6	1·8	2·5	2·5	2·7	2·8
West Midlands	0·9	1·3	2·5	2·2	2·0	2·3
North-West	1·6	1·5	2·5	2·5	2·5	2·8
Wales	2·6	2·9	4·1	4·0	4·1	4·0
Scotland	3·0	2·9	3·9	3·8	3·7	4·3
Northern Ireland	6·1	6·1	7·7	7·2	7·3	7·0

Source: Statistics for Economic Planning Regions from: Abstract of Regional Statistics No. 7, (H.M.S.O., London, 1972) Tables 21 & 26

Incomes

In earned income the status of Northern Ireland is as unenviable as in unemployment. Of all the regions of the United Kingdom, it has the lowest level of earnings and the highest percentage of households in the low income groups (Fig. 2).

In the financial year 1969–70 the average male earnings in Great Britain were £1369; in Northern Ireland they amounted to £1115, only 81·4 per cent of the mainland average and £113 less than East Anglia, the next lowest in the United Kingdom. The situation within individual employment categories was similar. In October 1970, male manual workers in manufacturing industry earned £25·43 per week in Northern Ireland, which amounted to only 88·0 per cent of the United Kingdom average of £28·91. Even in agriculture, which pays notoriously badly, wages in Northern Ireland are the lowest in the United Kingdom. In 1970 the national average agricultural wage was £18·49 per week; in Northern Ireland it was a mere £13·79 or 74·6 per cent of this.

The end result is that household incomes in Northern Ireland are the lowest in the country. In the financial year 1968–9 they amounted to £31·22 per household in the United Kingdom; in Northern Ireland the average household income was £27·18 (Fig. 2). In the same year 29 per cent of the households in the United Kingdom had a total income of less than £20 per week; in Northern Ireland the figure was 36 per cent.

Emigration

In view of the persistently high level of unemployment and the low wages compared with the rest of the United Kingdom, it is scarcely surprising that emigration is a traditional feature of Northern Irish life. During the period 1951–61 net movement outwards probably amounted to about 92 200 persons; between 1961 and 1966 it is estimated at just over 37 700 or about 6000 each year. In a single year 1965–6 gross emigration totalled 22 000 people. However, there is a substantial movement in as well as out. Over the same twelve months there were 15 100 immigrants, giving a net population loss of 6900. The consultants for the 1970–5 Development Programme estimated that over the period covered by their terms of reference the net loss of population by migration from Northern Ireland would be about 30 000.

The numbers, composition, destination, and motives of migrants are notoriously difficult to discover, but certain hypotheses would seem intuitively reasonable. In view of the foregoing discussion on levels of unemployment and income, it seems highly likely that the greater number and diversity of well-paid economic openings in Great Britain constitutes the prime motivation. It also seems likely that these emigrants will tend to be drawn particularly from the younger, better educated and qualified sections of the population. If this is true it is a serious loss, because it means Northern Ireland

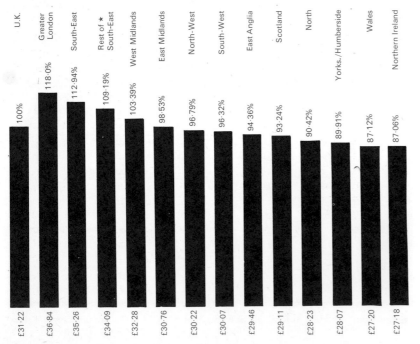

Fig. 2. Average household income 1968–9 (pounds per week and as proportion of U.K. average)

Source: *Abstract of Regional Statistics*, No. 7, 1971 (H.M.S.O. London, 1972)
* Not Standard Region

is losing that very section of her population which is best qualified in terms of age, ability, education, and innovative energy to tackle its serious economic and political problems.

However, several qualifications must be borne in mind when discussing loss by emigration. Firstly, the annual inflow of about 15 000 migrants, while it does not fully compensate for out-migration in numbers may do so in terms of characteristics. It seems highly likely that the vast majority of these immigrants originate in Great Britain and tend to be senior professional and managerial people, often coming to occupy key posts in new industries and administration. Secondly, no region is a totally closed system and every peripheral region like Northern Ireland must expect to lose a certain proportion of its better qualified population who move out to seek the highly specialized career openings rarely found in such small areas. Indeed, one could argue that it is surprising there is not more emigration from Northern Ireland. In the late 1950s in particular there was a period when unemployment in Northern Ireland was persistently over 7 per cent while the rest of the United Kingdom was experiencing a labour shortage. Despite the widespread diffusion of information about vacancies in the rest of the country and the absence of legislative barriers to movement, the emigration level remained low when compared with that of the Irish Republic. This may have been due to the relatively high level of welfare services in Northern Ireland compared with the Irish Republic, or perhaps the skills of the unemployed did not correspond with those most needed in Great Britain. Emigration from Northern Ireland is also relatively low when compared with recent losses from Scotland, which have been proportionately twice as high, and from the Northern Region of England where the outflow has also been much larger.

However, even allowing for all these considerations it remains true that Northern Ireland is sharing to some extent in that loss of labour, energy, and brain power which has characterized the peripheral regions of the United Kingdom in recent years and which they can ill afford to experience.

Causes of the problem

Structural weaknesses

One of the persistent causes of economic difficulty in Northern Ireland is that until the 1950s its economy was too narrowly based on manufacturing export industries, particularly marine engineering, shipbuilding, and textiles. Since then the world market for these goods has altered in response to changing demand patterns, the firms concerned have gone out of business or rationalized their operations and reduced their labour forces. Agriculture has undergone a similar period of readjustment with a shrinkage in its labour force. Unfortunately new economic activities have been less labour-intensive than the old and many have employed largely female labour forces which are still paid less than males. Consequently, while the decline in the older industries has continued, a largely male pool of surplus unemployed labour has persisted.

Until the early 1950s heavy manufacturing in Northern Ireland was dominated by **shipbuilding** and **marine engineering** and these two industries in turn were monopolized by the Harland and Wolff complex in Belfast. In 1950 they employed over 20 000 workers, providing more than 10 per cent of all manufacturing jobs in Northern Ireland and almost 20 per cent of those in Belfast. Approximately one-third of these jobs were in the marine engineering section.

By the early 1950s this Belfast branch of Harland and Wolff had established a notable record. It was the largest single shipbuilding yard in the world and on several occasions had topped the world league table for tonnage output by shipbuilding firms. Moreover, the complex at Belfast covered over 740 hectares, with 14 berths, several of which could easily build the largest ships of the time. There was a high level of activity during this period: in 1950 the Belfast firm launched 10 per cent of the gross tonnage launched in the United Kingdom; there was a good deal of fitting-out under way on recently completed naval vessels and work was just beginning on several new orders.

Since then, however, a variety of factors have arisen which have led to the steady contraction of the Belfast shipbuilding and marine engineering industry in both output and labour force. To some extent the Belfast yard merely shared the difficulties of the rest of the British industry, but there were some factors peculiar to it alone. Much of the post-1945 activity had been based on completion of wartime orders and replacement of naval and mercantile war losses. Moreover, during the war the shipyards of several potential competitors had been devastated and for several years afterwards, the defeated Axis powers were forbidden to engage in shipbuilding. Consequently, the British yards were one of the few suppliers still operating and Belfast shared to the full in these opportunities. The Korean War and general

Harland and Wolff Ltd., Belfast shipyards. The foundries and workshops are in the foreground; the recently completed dry dock and giant crane are in the centre, with the aircraft factory and airfield beyond

rearmament of the NATO powers prolonged this period of high activity into the mid-1950s.

By this time, however, new patterns of demand and competition began to emerge. Belfast had long specialized in the construction of large naval and mercantile vessels, especially aircraft carriers, passenger liners, and tankers. Demand for the first two began to fall off notably from the mid-1950s onwards and although Belfast increased its share of the growing demand for tankers, this was not sufficient compensation. Moreover, many of the foreign yards damaged by the war, had been reconstructed and both West Germany and Japan reappeared as competitors. Since these industries had been virtually rebuilt from nothing they were able to take advantage of the latest innovations and techniques in organization, layout, and construction. Consequently, competition for export markets became progressively greater and Belfast, along with other British yards, found its generally higher prices and more uncertain delivery dates were definite disadvantages. Bad labour relations, of which

Belfast had more than its share, contributed to these shortcomings. By the start of the 1960s world demand for new construction had declined considerably and in the intense competition for new orders the British yards often found their disadvantages fatal. Those contracts which were won were often obtained by desperate recourse to unremunerative prices which resulted in a number of years without profits. Not only were overseas orders being lost: even British shipowners found prices and construction times were less and delivery dates more reliable if they ordered from foreign builders.

By the late 1950s and early 1960s it was widely recognized in British shipbuilding that considerable modernization and rationalization were necessary if any part of the industry were to survive. The Belfast yards had suffered from changing circumstances as much as any in the United Kingdom and here too, radical readjustment was necessary. The number of berths was reduced by half, one yard was closed and another rebuilt to accommodate the increasing size of modern ships. Large amounts of new equipment, machinery, and heavy cranage were installed and considerable sums were directed to the construction of pre-frabrication facilities.

Alongside this process of consolidation and modernization steady decline in output set in during the early 1960s and has continued ever since. For the first time since 1945 output fell below 100 000 gross tons in 1962 and it has remained at around 80 000 gross tons each year since then. The structure of output also altered until, in order of importance by gross tonnage, tankers were most significant, followed by cargo vessels, passenger-cum-cargo vessels, passenger liners, and naval ships.

Such contraction of physical plant and output also involved notable shrinkage of the labour force. Up to 1960 the labour force had actually expanded slightly until it exceeded the level of employment in 1950. From 1960 to 1964, however, 11 500 jobs were lost in shipbuilding, repairing, and marine engineering. The process of contraction has continued, though on a less dramatic scale, until by mid-1972 only 10 000 were employed.

By the early 1960s therefore shipbuilding occupied a much less significant position in the economy of Northern Ireland than in 1950 or 1960 and it could easily be argued that, while the process of rationalization and contraction was a painful one, especially in view of the large-scale shedding of labour, it was a necessary first step towards widening the base of the regional economy.

Textiles in Northern Ireland have historically been dominated by the linen industry and all its associated activities. Here too there has been a period of adjustment over the past 20 years, which if anything has been even more radical and far-reaching than in shipbuilding and marine engineering. In fact the linen industry in the immediate post-war period was of considerably greater importance because by the early 1950s it employed about 60 000 people, one in three of Northern Ireland's manufacturing population and one in ten of the total employed. It also supplied the largest single group of items in the region's export pattern. The goods produced were generally craft-type luxury linens and to a much lesser extent, clothing. Unlike shipbuilding, this was not merely a further regional example of an industry found in other parts of the United Kingdom. The Northern Ireland linen industry was by far the largest in the country, unparalleled for the size of its labour force and output. Consequently, its decline over

the years has been particularly dramatic in national as well as regional terms. Here too however, it has suffered from forces world-wide, national, and regional in nature.

After the early 1950s the number of foreign markets shrank rapidly. This was due to various factors. Some countries deliberately restricted their import of 'luxury' linens, either because of currency restrictions or economy drives, or else because they wished to foster indigenous textile industries. Secondly, competition from cotton increased markedly. In part this was due to the fact that the British cotton industry, faced with broadly similar problems, had managed to re-organize itself much more quickly and efficiently. However, there was also growing competition from Asian cotton industries, permitted to sell relatively cheaply on the British market. Thirdly, man-made fibres began to appear in increasing variety and sophistication of design, colour, and texture and soon became a serious source of competition. Fourthly, changes in the economic structure of Northern Ireland had introduced new firms offering better wages and conditions and this made it increasingly difficult for the linen industry to retain its wage levels and working conditions. Finally, it seems more than likely that managerial attitudes during this period of increased competition resulted in many lost opportunities. The industry had traditionally been organized as a large number of small family firms whose management was inherited along with other family possessions. There was considerable pride in the production of a large variety of high quality craft products and deep-rooted opposition to modern methods of design, processing, manufacture, sale, and research. Management training was virtually unknown. In the American export market in particular these attitudes proved fatal. Some firms did try to adjust to the changed conditions by use of synthetic fibres and blends; several experimented with novel processes and products; some installed new equipment and others sought alternative markets. These, however, were exceptional and when the forces working against the linen industry reached a climax in the late 1950s there was considerable contraction in both labour force and manufacturing establishments. Over one-third of the plants closed down and 27 000 employees— over 45 per cent of the 1950 labour force—lost their jobs during the period 1958–64 alone.

The processes of adjustment experienced by these two major industries of shipbuilding and linen are perhaps two of the most dramatic in the United Kingdom. Probably no other regional

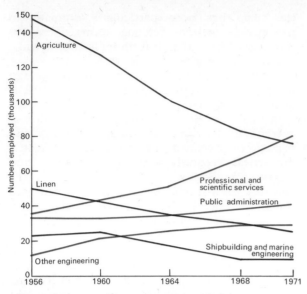

Fig. 3. Changes in employment structure 1956–71.
Statistics for agriculture include owners and their families

Source: Northern Ireland Digest of Statistics, September 1956,
1960, 1964, 1968, 1971

economy has had to undergo quite such a drastic alteration in its two manufacturing mainstays. Some idea of the scale of the process may be seen from the fact that in 1949 shipbuilding, linen, and their associated industries employed 55 per cent of the manufacturing workforce in Northern Ireland, whereas by 1970 the figure was less than 26 per cent.

Agriculture has also undergone a period of readjustment and contraction in recent years. Like shipbuilding, agriculture has been sharing in the experiences of the industry in the United Kingdom as a whole. Like shipbuilding, it occupied an unusually prominent position in the regional economy in post-war times, in this case employing over 22 per cent of the total labour force. The pattern of output and ownership was also distinctive. There was a strong emphasis on dairying and the production of oats, potatoes, poultry, and eggs. Most of the farms were owned and run on a family basis, employing very little outside labour, and by British standards were rather small.

The largest, indeed almost the only, market for Northern Ireland's agricultural produce is found in the rest of the United Kingdom and the nature of British demand together with national and regional government policies constitute the most important influences. In response to changing demand there has been a change of emphasis in Northern Irish farming from oats and potatoes towards pigs, barley (for pig food), and cattle for meat. To compete in the British market it was necessary for Northern Irish agriculture to become highly efficient. Consequently, considerable efforts were made to reduce the number of agricultural holdings, increase the size of individual farms, modernize buildings and techniques, introduce machinery, and educate the farm owner and workers in new attitudes and methods. Considerable encouragement, aid, and advice have been made available by the Northern Ireland Government. Thus over the years there has been much investment in the modernization of farm buildings, livestock, and equipment. The number of holdings has steadily diminished, with the result that very small farms have become steadily fewer and there has been a trend towards larger units. The size of the agricultural workforce has also fallen—from 148 370 in 1956 to 76 400 in 1971—so that only 13 per cent of the labour force is employed in agriculture. This process of contraction in total units and workforce has been accompanied by a steady expansion of total production, which rose by 2·5 per cent annually throughout the period 1964–70.

In many ways this has been a welcome change; rising agricultural production and productivity have accompanied a decline in the working population and the number of production units. However, there are certain qualifications. Firstly, despite the fall in number of very small farms, there are still too many remaining. Secondly, to some extent the figures suggesting increase in numbers of large units may be misleading since many farms appear to be enlarged by the process of conacre or seasonal letting rather than by outright purchase and amalgamation. Consequently, the basic problems of structure and ownership persist and the process of reducing workforce and total number of farms must continue if efficiency is to be increased and reasonable profits and incomes can be assured.

The continuing decline of these three former pillars of Northern Ireland's economy has in each case involved a radical reduction in the total labour force and therefore the release of considerable numbers onto the labour market. These structural changes do, therefore, go a long way towards explaining the region's chronic economic troubles but the factor of relative location may also be significant.

Relative location
It has often been implied that one of the great difficulties in attracting new economic activity to Northern Ireland is its peripheral location in relation to its sources of raw materials and

markets. On these grounds it is suggested that increasing distance involves notably increased costs which must be compensated either by lower profits or by higher prices which reduce competitiveness. In reply to this it has been argued that in fact it is not distance which adds significantly to costs but rather breaks of transport form, since they involve considerable inputs of time and labour. Consequently the physical barrier of the Irish Sea rather than simple travel time and distance becomes significant because two changes of transport form are necessary. But even here it would appear that only some types of goods are affected. It has been suggested that one of the disadvantages of the Belfast ship-building industry in the 1950s was the extra expense involved in shipment of steel from British works to Belfast. Similarly it is claimed that the necessity of importing farm materials such as animal foodstuffs from Great Britain adds to prices.

The real attraction of centrally located areas of the United Kingdom and Western Europe may be more in the internal economies of agglomeration, both real and imagined, which accrue from location in or close to existing concentrations of labour, expertise, information services, and all the existing economic, political, and social infrastructure so significant for modern economic growth. It is in this form therefore that Northern Ireland's relative location may be most disadvantageous.

High natural increase of population

Northern Ireland also faces problems created by the highest birth-rate in the United Kingdom. During most of the 1960s the birth-rate in Northern Ireland was just above 22 per 1000. In 1969 there was a fall to 21·4 and it is possible that unsettled political conditions and economic uncertainty since then may have kept it around this level. However, even allowing for this, the population increased faster by natural repro-duction alone than in any other part of the kingdom. In England and Wales the comparable rate was 16·3 and in Scotland 17·4 per 1000.

Two compensating factors at work are death-rate and emigration; but the death-rate of 10·8 per 1000 in 1969 was the lowest in the United Kingdom: comparative figures for England and Wales were 11·8 and for Scotland 12·3. The emigration levels already considered help to reduce the rate of increase but the inflow must also be recalled. However, even when due allowance is made for these factors, the total population of Northern Ireland was increasing by almost 10 000 each year during the first half of the 1960s and by 7000 yearly during the period 1966–71. Clearly this means a steady rise in the number of people seeking employment for the first time.

Attempted solutions

The situations outlined above provoked a variety of responses. Some firms attempted to continue with time-honoured methods and inevitably they were the first and most frequent victims of closure. Others attempted to rationalize and reorganize operations, utilized less labour, adopted new techniques in manufacture and marketing, and diversified into new branches or into entirely novel forms of output. In all these approaches to the situation the role of national and regional government has been highly significant. An elaborate system of inducements has arisen to attract new industry. Considerable efforts have also been made at all levels to improve transport facilities, particularly at the main ports of Belfast and Larne.

Aid to existing industries

The role of the British Government has been most notable as a source of funds for loans and grants aiding the readjustment of the aircraft and ship-building industries and also as a source of military orders for their end products. The Northern Ireland Government has also supplied funds on a generous but less spectacular scale. The aircraft industry in Northern Ireland originated shortly before the Second World War from a strategically motivated decision to decentralize military air-craft production away from more vulnerable parts of central and south-eastern England. The main factories are based in east Belfast with a small subsidiary in Newtownards, Co. Down. During the Second World War, Short Bros. and Harland specialized in production of flying boats and light reconnaissance and bombing aircraft. In post-war years airliners were also produced but the main emphasis has always been on military aircraft and related weapons systems. By the mid-1950s the labour force totalled 8–9000 workers. It seems highly likely that in an age of rising costs and increasing specialization and complexity of demand this relatively small firm would probably have gone out of business by the early 1960s. Various responses were forth-coming. The firm itself experimented with new types of aircraft and missiles. Some of the first successful trials in vertical take-off and landing were made; a large military freighter was produced together with a modified civil equivalent. None of these proved particularly successful, however, either because the company lacked the resources necessary to risk full-scale development of its innovations, or because its designs were too specialized and large-scale military or civil orders were simply not possible. The only really successful sales came from a series of military missiles which symbolized the firm's diversification into electronic and electrical goods and eventually even household appliances.

Soon after the Second World War the British Government had indicated its strong interest in the firm by aquisition of a 69·5 per cent holding. The motive for such a role may have been to prevent the break-up of the research and design team and the loss of valuable strategic skills and also to protect the regional economy from the effects of total closure. The Northern Ireland Government probably appreciated this last factor particularly strongly. Over the years this industry has received a significant level of military orders from the British Government. Even more notable, it has also been in receipt of a large number of loans and grants. Several of these have been for specific projects. Thus £2·5 million was granted by Westminster for production of the 'Skyvan' freighter and in late 1966 £510 000 was granted for completion of current orders for the Belfast freighter and two types of guided missiles. Altogether between 1963 and 1972 over £22 million was made available. Strenuous efforts have also been made to obtain sub-contracting work on large projects such as the RB2-11. Early in 1972 the British Government increased its orders for missiles, waived the interest on £2 million worth of loans and underwrote the production of further 'Skyvan' freighters.

The purpose of government aid to the shipbuilding industry has been to encourage reorganization on an economically sound basis to meet world competition. Once again a way of doing this is to provide temporary working capital over a short period. In 1966, for example, the Northern Ireland Government guaranteed a nine month loan of £1·5 million in a particularly difficult period. However, such measures have been much less significant than in the case of the aircraft industry. More frequently government action has been taken to help in the process of structural change by financing reorganization and re-equipment. Thus in April 1968 the Shipbuilding Industry Board made a loan of £8 million towards the estimated cost of £13·5 million for a new dry dock able to take the largest

ships then being contemplated. In all, this Board has granted £22·5 million to Harland and Wolff. Both Governments became actively interested again in late 1970 when losses of £3 775 000—later raised to £8 330 000—were announced for the year 1969. For a period of three months they assumed control of Harland and Wolff. The firm was returned to normal management in March 1971, but a new financial controller had been appointed. Four months later, large-scale reorganization was announced by the Northern Ireland Government. Four million pounds were spent in buying unissued ordinary shares which gave the Stormont Government a 47·6 per cent interest in the company; a new chairman and managing director were appointed; an existing short-term loan of £3·5 million from the Northern Ireland Government was converted to a long-term loan repayable over 33 years from 1974, and a fresh grant of £3 million was also made. Unfortunately this was not the end of Harland and Wolff's troubles. By early 1972 it became clear that record losses of over £14 million were likely for 1971, chiefly because the firm had been taking on contracts at unrealistically low prices simply to remain in operation and retain its workforce. In May 1972 the newly appointed Secretary of State for Northern Ireland announced an ambitious development programme for Belfast shipyards. As a first step, a British Government grant of over £14 million was advanced to wipe out recent losses. Beyond this there was to be £35 million worth of development over the next few years, including most notably an expansion of the workforce by 4000. A 'substantial proportion' of the funds for this was expected to come from the company's own resources.

Clearly therefore the survival of the Belfast shipbuilding industry in its present form is due in large measure to generous regional and national government aid. This differs somewhat from the aircraft industry's situation in both nature and aim. Whereas the motives in aiding the aircraft industry were largely strategic and social, in the case of the shipyards they are political and economic. Shipbuilding has been a staple of the Northern Irish economy for over 100 years and moreover its workforce has been and still is strongly Protestant and vehemently in favour of preserving the Union with Great Britain. The consequences of massive redundancies for the local economy and for the fortunes of the ruling Unionist Party in Belfast might have been considerable. After the imposition of direct rule at Easter 1972 the announcement of large-scale British government aid may have been designed to avoid the addition of large-scale economic discontent to an already volatile political situation.

In the case of the linen industry the regional government made similar though less direct efforts to encourage adaptation to changing conditions of demand and competition. Here the chief forms of aid lay in the setting up of a Linen Industry Research Association just outside Belfast to encourage experiments and innovation in all aspects of linen manufacture and production. Between 1951 and 1960 it was estimated that £18 million were spent on capital replacements and improvements, largely under the impetus of government aided schemes. Unfortunately it seems the industry did not respond with sufficient alacrity to these opportunities. This may have been due to the fact that it was still organized on the basis of a large number of small family firms which had been in the trade for centuries. Their emphasis on individualistic and traditional craft approaches to manufacture, management, and sales rendered them slow to accept and experiment with new ideas. Consequently the application of government aid and research findings was slow and patchy, and this may go far to explain the rapid contraction of the industry in the late 1950s and early 1960s.

In agriculture the situation has been very different. Here the regional government has gone to considerable lengths to encourage the re-organization of farming for greater production and all-round efficiency. The agricultural community responded readily and has taken up the facilities offered to aid modernization. The government aim was to encourage efficient high quality dairy production for the British market, thereby ensuring reasonable and secure incomes for the agricultural community. To this end considerable incentive schemes were made available to encourage eradication of small uneconomic holdings by amalgamation into larger units. Modernization of plant and equipment was also encouraged. Considerable efforts were made to connect all farms to mains electricity, and this was largely achieved by the late 1960s. Mechanization was encouraged and by the early 1970s the ownership of tractors was commonplace and almost £5 million was tied up in such equipment. A complex system of grants and subsidies was introduced to encourage improvements in farm housing and building, drainage, sewage disposal, access roads, land reclamation, provision of livestock pens and fences, and farm management. There are also Remoteness Grants from the United Kingdom Government to help overcome the disadvantage of peripheral location *vis à vis* the main British markets. Considerable efforts are also made to up-grade the quality of livestock herds by government organized selective breeding together with rigorous import controls and constant inspection and certification to ensure freedom from disease. Marketing of all livestock and cereal products is equally carefully controlled. Alongside all these services, agricultural education, advice, and research are also highly organized.

It has been largely due to the availability of such services plus the pressures of market demand that agriculture in Northern Ireland has notably increased its total output and productivity while reducing the total number of production units and the labour force.

Attraction of new industries

Considerable efforts have been made to attract entirely new forms of economic activity. To this end there are two main types of aid available. Under a series of Industries Development (N.I.) Acts, the Ministry of Commerce was able to offer assistance for projects creating additional employment. The amount and type of assistance are negotiated individually with due consideration being given to employment provided, location of project, and extent to which it helps diversify the industrial structure. Manufacturing firms may receive grants of up to 50 per cent of the cost of factory buildings and 45 per cent if they are already established in Northern Ireland and wishing to expand further. Grants are offered towards capital expenditure on plant, machinery, and buildings by firms in the manufacturing, extractive, and construction industries. Grants are also available for consulting advice on improving efficiency and for management training, together with loans for modernization and re-equipment. In addition to this there are schemes of government-provided factories and standard advance factories.

During the period 1964–9 over 28 800 new jobs were created in manufacturing alone by the establishment of new industry, and the Government of Northern Ireland provided some form of assistance in the establishment of each new and expanded plant. During the same period there were undoubtedly other factors working in favour of Northern Ireland. Firstly, the British Board of Trade was operating a system of Industrial Development Certificates which it often withheld from firms wishing to set up in the South-East or the West Midlands of England. Secondly, when such establishments sought

TABLE 2
Percentages of total employees in selected economic activities, June 1970

	U.K.	North	Yorks, Humber	East Midlands	East Anglia	South-East	South-West	West Midlands	North-West	Wales	Scotland	N. Ireland
Total in all industries and services (in thousands)	22 891	1270	1976	1392	637	7698	1310	2259	2842	935	2077	487
Agric., forestry, fisheries	1·7	1·5	1·5	2·2	8·0	1·2	2·9	1·2	0·5	1·4	2·8	1·8
Food, drink, tobacco	3·9	3·2	4·5	3·7	7·1	3·0	5·1	3·3	4·7	2·4	5·3	6·0
Shipbuilding, marine engineering	0·9	3·1	0·4	0·1	0·6	0·5	1·4	0·0	1·0	0·2	2·1	2·1
Vehicles	3·7	1·1	2·5	4·0	3·3	3·0	4·7	9·5	4·3	2·6	2·0	1·6
Textiles	3·1	1·9	7·8	8·6	0·6	0·4	1·1	1·5	6·4	2·0	4·1	8·8
Clothing and footwear	2·2	2·8	2·9	5·0	1·9	1·6	1·9	0·9	2·9	1·7	1·5	5·5
Paper, printing, and publishing	2·9	1·5	1·9	1·9	2·8	4·1	3·0	1·5	3·2	1·5	2·7	1·4
Total mnfg. industries	38·9	38·2	43·6	45·5	34·1	32·4	32·7	53·5	46·0	37·2	35·6	37·8
Transport, communications	7·0	5·7	6·0	4·7	6·4	8·6	6·3	4·7	7·3	6·7	6·9	4·9
Distributive trades	11·8	11·6	11·1	11·0	11·5	13·0	12·8	9·1	11·8	9·9	12·5	11·3
Insurance, banking, finance, and business services	4·2	2·0	2·6	2·2	2·5	7·4	2·8	2·4	3·1	2·0	2·9	2·1
Professional and scientific services	12·6	12·4	11·9	10·8	13·2	13·1	14·4	10·8	12·0	13·4	13·7	14·4
Miscellaneous services	8·1	8·1	6·8	6·0	9·1	9·4	10·5	5·9	6·9	7·5	8·0	7·8
Public administration and defence	6·2	6·4	4·6	4·7	6·0	7·6	7·5	4·3	4·8	7·0	5·8	8·0

Source : Statistics for Economic Planning Regions from: Abstract of Regional Statistics, No. 7 (H.M.S.O., London, 1972), Table 22

locations elsewhere it may have been the pool of unemployed labour in Northern Ireland which attracted their attention. The chief significance of the inducements offered by the regional government lay in the fact that they were always marginally more generous than those available for Development Areas in Great Britain. As such their chief effect was marginally to reduce capital costs. It has been estimated that a typical light engineering firm setting up in Northern Ireland would receive assistance equivalent to about 4 per cent of the value of gross output or 7 per cent net output. Clearly this is a relatively small amount, though as a proportion of net profits it may be much greater. Furthermore, it may be particularly helpful in strengthening the liquidity position of a new firm during the initial stages of establishment and growth. It is probably during such early stages that the considerable range of inducements, services, and advice available, plus the ease and rapidity of contact with officials of the regional administration, are most decisive as locational factors.

The impact of all these factors on the detailed economic structure of Northern Ireland has been considerable. By the late 1960s about one-third of all manufacturing employment was in jobs provided by plants set up since 1950. During the 1950s about half of the new jobs were created by the expansion of long-established existing industries such as tobacco, clothing, textiles, engineering, and mechanical engineering. During the 1960s, however, the emphasis was very much on the establishment of completely new forms of economic activity. The most notable were branches of the light engineering, electronics, and man-made fibres industries (Fig. 3). These were particularly welcome for two reasons. They represented an entirely novel element in the regional economy and thus helped to broaden it considerably. Furthermore their products were of high value and small bulk and thus were able to sustain the difficulties of long distance transfer to market. There was also a notable contribution by new firms manufacturing ladies' and children's clothing and processing agricultural produce.

Eighty-five per cent of the incoming plants originated from Great Britain and the remaining 15 per cent were mostly of American origin. These foreign-established concerns tended to be the largest while the 10 per cent established by local enterprise were usually the smallest. The end result of this process of economic readjustment was that by the early 1970s the economic structure of Northern Ireland was basically much sounder than twenty years before. The earlier, dangerously narrow dependence on shipbuilding and traditional textiles had been considerably lessened to the point where instead of employing over 55 per cent of the manufacturing workforce as in 1949, by 1970 the figure was less than 26 per cent. There was still a strong textile emphasis, but it was made up of expanding modern synthetic fibre plants rather than factories producing traditional craft-based luxury linens. The shipbuilding industry had contracted and was re-equipping itself. Most encouraging of all, there had been a continuous process of expansion and diversification into highly sophisticated electrical and electronic engineering industries.

Port and harbour improvements

In order to overcome some of the difficulties posed by Northern Ireland's peripheral location and physical separation from the rest of the United Kingdom, considerable efforts have been made to modernize its main ports of Belfast and Larne. The port of Belfast is very much man-made and constant improvement has to be maintained by the Harbour Authority. A recently completed £14 million development scheme has given the port a total dock area of 990 hectares. Ships of up to 50 000 tons can be accommodated. In all there are 73 berths with 13 kilometres of quayside, and dockside sheds covering 13 hectares. Three of the berths are reserved for freight services with Great Britain alone. Glasgow, Heysham, and Liverpool have daily freight and passenger services with Belfast and there are regular freight services connecting with eight other British ports plus scheduled services to Western Europe, the Middle East, Canada, and

the U.S.A. Vehicle and container ferry services have also been introduced on a large scale.

The most notable container port is Larne in Co. Antrim. Growth here has been remarkably rapid and is largely explained by its specialization in wheeled vehicle and container traffic for which there are three large specially built berths with modern vehicle ramps. The particular advantages of these forms of transport are that the retention of goods in container form enables a smooth and easy transfer from one form of transport to another with minimum handling of the goods concerned. There are now regular passenger ferry and container services from Larne to Stranraer, Preston, Ardrossan, and Antwerp.

Conclusion

There is little doubt that considerable progress has been made over the past 20 years in broadening the base of Northern Ireland's economy (Table 2) and the roles of national and regional government have been highly significant, particularly in shipbuilding and agriculture. However, there are also certain problems remaining. In the case of aircraft it must be questioned whether a small firm with such slender resources can have a secure long-term future independent of government aid in an industry where the cost and scale of projects are accelerating so rapidly that only massive corporations and international consortia can operate on a truly economic basis. The future of this industry in Northern Ireland, dependent as it is on government cash contracts and subcontracting work, is rather dubious. Shipbuilding is in a somewhat happier position. It is true that in recent years it has taken on too many fixed-price contracts at unrealistically low prices. However, much work on such projects has been completed and there is every indication that future policy is to avoid repetition of such errors. Moreover, there has been considerable modernization of plant and equipment and the plans announced in mid-1972 suggested this to be an ongoing process. A further encouraging sign was the construction of an oil drilling rig in the mid-1960s, experience which may enable the firm to attract more work of this nature as exploration and exploitation of North Sea resources continue. One difficulty which must be faced, however, is the reorganization of the rest of the British industry into a small number of large consortia. If a position akin to that of the aircraft industry is to be avoided, a relationship with one of the large British groupings would seem necessary. Farming is probably the sector of the economy which has performed best in recent years. However, this progress must be maintained if the industry is to retain its share in the highly competitive British market. In particular, the persistently high number of very small and unviable holdings will have to be reduced by sale and genuine amalgamation rather than by conacre, and consideration will have to be given to the extra costs imposed by importation of animal foodstuffs from Great Britain.

Certain features of the new industries also give cause for concern. One difficulty is that the rate of creation of new jobs in recent years has not kept pace with the release of labour from the old established industries. In particular, agriculture has been shedding labour at a much faster rate than expected. Further, it was believed that in the period 1964 to 1969, service employment would expand and provide 30 000 new openings. Unfortunately only 13 000 appeared, largely due to national government curbs on consumer spending and the imposition of a Selective Employment Tax designed to slow down growth in service industries. The abolition of S.E.T. and an unexpectedly rapid expansion in the construction industry may help to offset this, but there is considerable leeway to be made up.

A second difficulty is the fact that many of the new industries established are intensive of capital rather than labour. This is particularly the case in the synthetic fibres and sophisticated engineering sectors. Consequently, while the high value of their end products gives Northern Ireland a higher value per capita domestic product than any other region of the United Kingdom, they provide fewer openings than the less capital-intensive older industries.

Further, the nature of the labour needs of the new activities do not correspond to the nature of the pool of unemployed available. The workers being released by the contracting industries are males who possess traditional manufacturing or agricultural skills and are often well advanced in years. Unfortunately many of the new industries are best suited to younger females with minimal skills or else to younger men skilled in light engineering. New skills can be imparted by the extensive and ambitious schemes of industrial training sponsored by the regional government. The difficulties imposed by age and sex are less easily surmounted. Indeed, so intense has the competition for female labour become that in some areas it is actually in short supply while in the same districts there is a chronically high level of male unemployment. Since in many households the women are the wage earners and since they usually earn less than men, the problem of low household incomes persists and may indeed be growing. It remains necessary therefore to attract new industries which can employ large numbers of males who at present have traditional skills or none at all.

A further disturbing feature about the new industries is that so many are branches of British or foreign concerns and less than 10 per cent were founded by local initiative. This suggests that decisions about the level and future of operations will be taken in London, Birmingham, or New York rather than in Belfast and will not be influenced by local people or considerations of the likely impact of contraction and closure on the local and regional economies. Such a situation often provokes unease and insecurity in the region concerned. However, it does mean that decisions are more likely to be based on strictly economic arguments and in the long run this may result in a more soundly based economy. Another thought suggested is that local entrepreneurship in Northern Ireland appears to be at low ebb. Its contribution to economic development in recent decades has been largely confined to extension of existing industries such as tobacco and food processing. In view of the past record of local entrepreneurship this is difficult to explain, although emigration must be taken into account.

A final difficulty is one which the consultants at work on the Development Programme for 1970–5 described as 'the political condition of the province'. The actual long-term physical damage done to industry during the disturbances which began in 1968 was minimal. It was largely confined to one or two old factories in west Belfast and a number of retail and wholesale outlets in central Belfast and Londonderry. Most of these were in operation again within a few months. However, the dramatic impact of the disturbances and the doubts about the long-term political future of the province must have seriously eroded the confidence of those most likely to be considering investment and economic activity in Northern Ireland. Until this question is settled future economic progress is likely to be impaired. The complexities of the political problem are such as to demand separate treatment in depth.

3 The Political Problem

The nature of the problem

The political problems of Northern Ireland are less easily understood than the economic ones and, unlike the latter, are probably without parallel in contemporary British and European affairs. In many respects they are more reminiscent of nineteenth-century Europe or indeed the alignment of European and British politics in the sixteenth and seventeenth centuries.

In Northern Ireland the chief political issue is the nature and purpose of the State itself. The legitimacy of the existing constitutional and political arrangements is fiercely disputed by a significant minority of the population. Moreover, the dispute is not merely over who has the right to rule or in what fashion. The dispute is basically a question of national identity. Of the total population of approximately 1·5 million, about two-thirds see themselves as being British. Consequently they vehemently support the existing constitutional links under which Northern Ireland has always been part of the United Kingdom. Since the late nineteenth century they have consistently supported the Ulster Unionist Party in elections to local councils, the regional Parliament at Stormont, and the British Parliament at Westminster, because this party has always made preservation of the Union with Britain its chief electoral plank.

The remaining one-third of the population see themselves as being Irish. Consequently, their personal and political loyalties have always been to the neighbouring Irish Republic (Eire) comprising the remaining 26 counties of Ireland. Since the early nineteenth century they have supported a series of political parties designed to express Irish national feelings. During the period when Britain and all of Ireland comprised the United Kingdom, the Irish Home Rule and later the Nationalist Party was the chief vehicle for the articulation of Irish national sentiments, both Northern and Southern. Early in the present century the political initiative passed to the ultra-nationalistic Sinn Fein ('ourselves alone') which campaigned for a much greater degree of Irish independence. Following the Partition of Ireland in 1920 those in the six counties of Northern Ireland who opposed the retention of British rule in the north-east have given their support to a series of Irish Nationalist and independent Republican candidates of various types at all elections for local councils and for the Stormont and Westminster Parliaments. Throughout most of the modern era the chief political aim of this community and their public representatives has been to end the constitutional link (or Union) between Northern Ireland and the rest of the United Kingdom and to unite the six counties of Northern Ireland with the Irish Republic.

In such a situation where the very basics of constitutional and political arrangements are disputed, the forms and conventions of political life regarded as 'normal' in the rest of the United Kingdom are not present. In Great Britain, despite genuine differences in the outlook and the electoral bases of the main parties, there is also considerable room for compromise and it is fairly easy to discover a broad area of agreement or 'consensus' on what is desirable and necessary for purposes of sound and fair government. Moreover in British politics the basic political cleavage is on socio-economic lines associated with the production, utilization, and distribution of material wealth. Consequently the basic issues are such matters as wages, prices, housing, and health and welfare services. The existing constitutional arrangements are not called in question by any of the major parties, nor is the nature and philosophy of the State.

In Northern Ireland, however, consensus and compromise are extremely difficult, if not impossible. Indeed, so diametrically opposed are the two groups and so rigidly are the lines of loyalty drawn, that there is no 'swing' of voters at elections, as there has been throughout modern British politics. Consequently, the Unionist group have had a strong controlling majority and have formed the Government in the regional Parliament throughout Northern Ireland's history. The minority Irish Nationalists and Republicans have therefore comprised a permanent Opposition with no hope of coming to power. The cleavages have run so deep into the political fabric of Northern Ireland and proved so irreconcilable that politically inspired violence has become a traditional means of dealing with opponents.

The contrast with British political life could hardly be more total. In terms of European political geography the situation is only slightly less anomalous. Disputes over national identity, minorities, and boundaries did indeed comprise the basis of European politics for a time, but this era may be regarded as having finally ended with the treaties after the Second World War, when there were considerable exchanges of population and redrawing of boundaries, especially in Central and Eastern Europe. Today the basic issues of European affairs are probably associated with defence, economic development, and regional cooperation. Only in Yugoslavia, Germany, Poland, and, more openly, in South Tyrol, do questions of national minorities and boundary disputes still exacerbate relations between peoples.

The Northern Ireland question is rendered still more unusual by the fact that the distinguishing cultural characteristic of the two groups in conflict is their religion. Almost all of the one million people who regard themselves as British and support the continuation of the constitutional link with Great Britain are Protestant, chiefly Presbyterian and Anglican. By contrast, almost all of those who regard themselves as Irish and wish to see the unification of the six counties with the Irish Republic are Roman Catholic. Moreover, these denominational allegiances are associated with a much higher degree of theological orthodoxy and regular worship than is found in Great Britain. Since the early twentieth century religious belief and orthodoxy have declined sharply in British society where only a small minority of the population are regular church attenders. Parallel with these developments, religion as a dividing force has virtually disappeared from British political life. Although its influence can still be discerned as a rather minor factor in electoral behaviour, this may equally be a function of the age and of the social background as much as of the religious adherence of the electors.

In terms of West European politics Northern Ireland is almost equally anachronistic. Here, however, there are large Christian Democrat Catholic parties in several countries, notably Italy, West Germany, and the Netherlands and the Gaullists in France have a strong Roman Catholic base. But this is only one element in the political life of the countries concerned: only in the Netherlands are there Protestant-based competing parties and, moreover, religious loyalties are not associated with contending national ideologies. To find the best parallel with the clash of nationalities and sectarian groups in Northern Ireland one must turn to the political geography of post-Reformation France and Germany in the sixteenth and seventeenth centuries.

Causes of the problem

As a political unit Northern Ireland is something of an anomaly. While it is politically part of the United Kingdom, it is separated physically by at least 35 kilometres of water. It is the only part of the United Kingdom which has an international land boundary with a foreign country. Finally, only in this part of the United Kingdom is there a substantial national minority which rejects British citizenship and wishes adherence to another nation. The situation is equally anomalous when viewed from the Irish Republic. The six north-eastern counties of the island are the only part still under British jurisdiction. Moreover, this is the only part of the island which did not give enthusiastic support to the various Irish national movements but preferred to remain under British rule. Further, it is the only large area which does not share the overwhelmingly Roman Catholic religious adherence of the rest of Ireland and it is the only part which fully experienced the Industrial Revolution.

The origins of this regional differentiation of the north-east are deeply rooted in the historical geography of the island. One of the most ironic features of the Northern Ireland situation is the fact that this area, most of whose inhabitants now fervently claim to be British, was the region where traditional Gaelic Ireland survived longest in its most vigorous and undiluted form. Here the Norman impact had been confined to the coastal fringes of modern Down and Antrim. The collapse of Norman influence there was thus particularly rapid and by the mid-fourteenth century it was totally excluded from all the nine counties of Ulster (Fig. 4), save for a few small urban enclaves such as Downpatrick and Carrickfergus. When the English Tudor monarchs finally decided to extend their authority beyond the Dublin region to all of Ireland and to colonize it with reliable settlers, the north was the last area to be tackled. This was partly because Gaelic Irish military and social organization was still strongest there. It was also to some extent because such a vigorous people could make full use of the woodlands, lakes, mountains, and marshy areas which were found in the north in order to defend themselves.

While the nine counties of Ulster were the last to be conquered and settled, they were also the region where the process was most successful and long-lasting. For this reason much of the distinctive human geography of modern Northern Ireland must be traced back to this early seventeenth-century period of subjugation and settlement. Two of the historic nine Ulster counties— Antrim and Down—had already been the scene of much Scottish immigration in the sixteenth century and small parts of Monaghan were also settled. Most attention was concentrated on the remaining six counties, which were colonized by settlers from England and Scotland in a process known as the Plantation of Ulster. Previously this part of Ireland, like the rest of the country, had been Gaelic-speaking, Roman Catholic, rural-dwelling, and agricultural. Thirty-five towns were founded to act as garrison points and to civilize the surrounding rural areas by the diffusion of peaceful habits of sedentary living and commerce. The most fertile and accessible parts of their hinterlands were given over to agricultural development by further groups of Protestant colonists and the newly planted towns were intended to act as their market centres. These basic ideas were by no means novel. They has also been attempted in parts of Leinster and Munster. However, only the Plantation of Ulster has proved to be a successful and long-lasting venture. There are various reasons for this. First, there was a considerable difference in scale compared with previous efforts. The Leinster Plantation in particular was on a very limited basis— only the modern counties of Leix and Offaly were affected. In Munster it was rather more ambitious, but in Ulster it was most elaborate of all. Here the whole enterprise was much more thoroughly organized, executed, and soundly financed than before, perhaps on the basis of previous experience. Secondly, while actual figures for the numbers of settlers are hard to find, it does seem likely that far more were involved in Ulster than in previous Plantations. Thirdly, total military defeat of the Ulster chieftains had been followed by the flight to Catholic Europe of much of the Gaelic aristocracy thus depriving the population of their natural leaders who also forfeited all rights to their lands and property. In this way larger areas of land were available for confiscation and settlement. Finally, many of the previous attempts at settlement had gone awry because the settlers had intermarried with the Irish. In the case of the Ulster Plantation, however, this was less necessary and less likely because of their larger numbers and much greater degree of spatial concentration. Even more of a deterrent was the religious difference between the new settlers and the native Irish. The Reformation had converted most of Great Britain to Protestantism and left the Irish staunchly Roman Catholic. In an age when religious divisions ran much deeper than in contemporary Britain and were associated with more fervently held political attitudes, such differences were a powerful

obstacle to any miscegenation. When reinforced by the fact that the Planters were also alien in origin, culture, technology, and language they made assimilation almost impossible. In this way there was established that basic cleavage on grounds of nationality and religion which has persisted in north-east Ireland until the present.

From the early seventeenth to the early twentieth century the Protestant community comprised the social, economic, and political élite of Ireland. But only in Ulster, and especially in the six north-eastern counties, were Protestants to be found in a numerical majority at every level of society instead of being merely an aristocratic and professional minority. Here they were weavers, farmers, farm hands, and merchants instead of being confined to the ranks of clergy, professional men, and landowners. The Protestant community of the north-east was distinctive in origin and denomination as well as numbers. This is the part of Ireland closest to Scotland, and throughout the preceding centuries there had been considerable circulation of population across the North Channel. It will be recalled that large areas of Antrim and Down had been settled by Scots several decades before the Ulster Plantation proper. There was also a notable Scottish element amongst the Planters. Moreover, many of the colonists' losses sustained in the insurrections of 1641–8 and 1688–90 were replenished from Scotland.

The impact of the Scots on this part of Ireland has been felt in almost every aspect of life. The characteristic Ulster accent owes much to Scottish influence, and in some parts of County Antrim it can easily be mistaken for a Scots dialect. Presbyterianism, the largest Protestant denomination in Northern Ireland, is also a Scottish import, and relations between the Presbyterian Churches in Ireland and Scotland are still particularly close. The Scots settlers brought certain customs which were to have profound consequences for the economic life of Ulster. They brought with them a set of conventions relating to land-holding which were diffused throughout the entire Protestant community in the north-east and were referred to as 'Ulster Tenant Right'. Under these customs the Ulster tenant farmer was not a tenant-at-will without security, as were the vast majority in the rest of Ireland. Long leases were the almost universal rule in Ulster, thus providing the incentive of security for the tenant to improve his holding and his techniques. Moreover, if a tenant were evicted at the expiry of a lease he could claim compensation for any improvements made during his tenancy. Again, he was able to sell his interest in his holding and realize cash for it if he wished. Finally, amongst the farming community of the north-east, inheritance of land and property was by law of primogeniture—i.e. eldest son inherited all.

The Industrial Revolution too affected only the extreme north-east and left the rest of the island virtually untouched. To some extent this may be because it is the part of Ireland closest to Scotland and consequently the contemporary movement towards industrialization in the Clyde Valley may have 'spilled over' into Ulster. Certainly there was a good deal of Scottish capital in early Ulster industry and some of the leading entrepreneurs were recent Scots immigrants. It also seems likely that certain of the Scottish cultural and social customs introduced into Ulster may have been conducive to rapid economic progress. The traditions of land-holding referred to earlier probably made for more stable and relaxed social relations between landlord and tenant than elsewhere in Ireland. This in turn may have created an atmosphere of greater social and political stability which permitted and encouraged continuous economic growth and risk-taking. It is also possible that the Presbyterian ethos with its emphasis on literacy, self-discipline, hard work, and scrupulous care in financial dealing was conducive to shrewd decision-making, successful economic progress, and rapid capital accumulation.

Finally, the north-east was the scene of the earliest large-scale textile industry in Ireland, namely the linen industry. To some extent its location there was due to chance. A number of French Hugenot refugees had settled in the Protestant north-east and brought with them traditions of flax cultivation and linen manufacture. The crop and the associated cottage industries of spinning and weaving took hold rapidly in Ulster, where they were also combined with the cultivation of smallholdings. The result was a considerable broadening of the basically agricultural economy to incorporate an extra crop and a supplementary economic activity. It also meant the beginnings of a valuable tradition of skilled textile working. Further, the linen yarn and cloth had to be processed, dyed, and traded, which necessitated the manufacture of hand-powered machinery, chemicals, and tools and the organization of linen markets and fairs. Consequently, when Great Britain and particularly Scotland embarked on the Industrial Revolution, it was the north-east of Ireland that was best placed in terms of location, general

social conditions, inherited manual and entrepreneurial skills, and accumulated capital.

This regional economic differentiation became more marked as industrial activity expanded during the nineteenth century. A factory-based cotton industry grew up and soon afterwards linen took on the factory system as well. These textile industries were soon followed by the arrival of shipbuilding, ship-repairing, marine engineering, rope-making, and the processing of imported flour, sugar, animal foodstuffs, tobacco, and alcohol. The eastern towns of Ulster and the Belfast region in particular became the industrial core of Ireland. By the end of the nineteenth century, therefore, a significant part of the north-east had diverged even further from the rest of the country, reinforcing its social, cultural, and religious distinctiveness with a marked economic individuality based on textiles, heavy manufacturing, and processing industries. In its economic structure eastern Ulster resembled a region of Great Britain more than any part of Ireland.

In partisan political terms Ulster diverged equally sharply from the rest of Ireland as the nineteenth century progressed. During the century which followed the victory of William III at the Boyne in 1690 and the imposition of the Penal Laws, the Anglican ascendancy was not challenged. But in the 1790s Ireland became infected with the ideals of the French Revolution and in 1798 there was a limited but bloody insurrection by both Catholic and Protestant Dissenters. This was put down after severe fighting. Subsequently in 1800 the Irish Parliament was abolished by an Act of Union which united the two kingdoms under the British Crown.

As the nineteenth century developed, the identity of interest which the Protestant Dissenters had shared with the Catholic Irish in 1798 was rapidly eroded and on most political issues they became more and more identified with the Anglicans. This process of realignment was completed by the 1840s and when this happened political cleavages in Ireland became the sectarian Protestant versus Catholic conflict. Since the vast majority of Protestants were to be found in the north-east, this also meant that such political cleavages were as regional in their bases as the economic contrasts.

Throughout the nineteenth century the process of polarization continued. The basic Protestant conviction was that an Irish Parliament in Dublin would inevitably reflect the outlook and values of the Catholic faith professed by almost all the Irish population outside the north-east and that as a result Protestants would be relegated to second-class citizenship. Moreover, the industrial development of the north-east was by now well under way and it was feared that it would be seriously damaged by Home Rule for Ireland. The economic interests of Ulster would be best served by free trade and maximum contact with the rest of the British Isles, but it was believed that an Irish Parliament would be dominated in its economic thinking by the rural and agricultural nature of the rest of Ireland. This, it was feared, could easily lead it to adopt a protectionist policy to help its embryonic industries, thereby perhaps provoking retaliation against manufactured goods which the north-east generally marketed in Great Britain.

When Irish Nationalist activity for Home Rule came to the fore in the 1870s the vast majority of Southern Irish electors voted for the newly emergent Irish parliamentary party under first Butt and then Parnell. The entire Protestant north-east held aloof from the movement however. In 1886 when Gladstone and a large section of the Liberal Party took up the cause of Home Rule and introduced a Bill to this end, the north-eastern counties began to move towards the Conservative Unionism which has been their characteristic political outlook ever since (Fig. 4).

The polarization was, if possible, increased by the 1916 Rebellion in the Dublin area when certain Irish Republican elements took the opportunity of British preoccupation with the war to establish a provisional Irish Republic. The attempt failed after a few days but the vigorous manner of its suppression stimulated a tremendous upsurge of support for the Republican movement and its military wing, known as the Irish Republican Army (I.R.A.). This culminated in a massive electoral victory in 1918 when their political party Sinn Fein won almost every parliamentary seat in Southern Ireland and several in the Catholic areas of southern and western Ulster. The remaining areas of Ulster voted overwhelmingly Unionist. The political philosophies and views of the two communities in Ireland were now so totally at variance that they could not be contained within a single political area and it was from this position of impasse that in 1920 the decision was taken to partition Ireland.

The original scheme was to grant not one but two Home Rule Parliaments to Ireland: one in Dublin was to have jurisdiction over 26 counties, and another in Belfast over the six most strongly Protestant and Unionist counties. There was also to be a council of Ireland to coordinate policy on such matters as railways and fisheries and it was hoped that it would provide a forum for the gradual coming together of the two parts of the country. However, Southern Irish opinion had moved to the point where a much greater degree of independence than mere Home Rule was the aim. Consequently, the offer of a Home Rule Parliament in Dublin was rejected together with the Council of Ireland.

The result was that the six counties of the north-east were left with a Home Rule Parliament centred in Belfast. This had certainly not been the original Unionist goal. They had aimed at the retention of all of Ireland within the United Kingdom and their acceptance of the 1920 compromise of two Home Rule assemblies was grudging at best. Consequently, when Southern Ireland eventually signed a treaty with Great Britain in 1921, achieved Dominion status and later became a Republic outside the Commonwealth, the six counties of Northern Ireland remained within the United Kingdom but with a measure of regional devolution.

Unfortunately, however, 1920 was a less than perfect partition. The area to be partitioned off was chosen for reasons of political and administrative convenience. If all the nine counties of the historic province of Ulster had been chosen, it was believed there would probably be an almost equal number of Catholics and Protestants. It seems highly likely that this was the motive for the exclusion of the three most Catholic counties of Donegal, Cavan and Monaghan. In the six remaining counties it was estimated the Unionists could be assured of a firm working majority. It was originally intended that there should be a Boundary Commission appointed to adjust the border in accordance with local loyalties and aspirations, but shortly before it was due to publish its report in November 1925 a substantially accurate summary of its recommendations was 'leaked' to the press and because of the subsequent political uproar the report was shelved and the existing border accepted. In this way, boundaries originally drawn up in Elizabethan times for the purpose of delimiting judicial jurisdictions, were advanced to the status of disputed international boundaries.

For many reasons it was unfortunate that some readjustment of the boundary line was not attempted. At the very simplest level there are some particularly sinuous stretches between County Fermanagh and Cavan and Monaghan where the precise alignment has never been fully delimited or demarcated. In normal circumstances

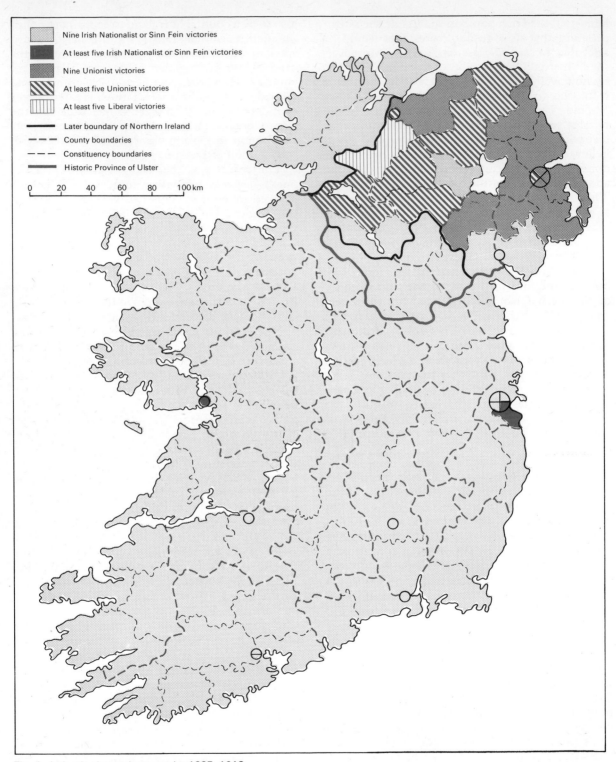

Nine Irish Nationalist or Sinn Fein victories

At least five Irish Nationalist or Sinn Fein victories

Nine Unionist victories

At least five Unionist victories

At least five Liberal victories

———— Later boundary of Northern Ireland

– – – County boundaries

– · – Constituency boundaries

━━━ Historic Province of Ulster

0   20   40   60   80   100 km

Fig. 4. Ireland: electoral geography 1885–1918

this can render the operation of customs juris-diction extremely difficult. In times of political tension and terrorist activity it can result in unintentional border crossings with tragic and far-reaching political consequences. From an eco-nomic viewpoint the border cut several large settlements off from their normal hinterlands. Londonderry and Newry suffered most seriously because both had been ports with a considerable handling and distribution function for large areas of Donegal, and Cavan and Louth respectively. When added to their problems of peripheral location in relation to the largest centre of wealth, market, and labour in Northern Ireland, the result has been to exacerbate their chronic economic difficulties. As far as Northern Ireland as a whole is concerned, however, the most far-reaching result of Partition has been that it did not reflect the precise spatial distribution of the pro-Union and pro-Nationalist populations. Within the six counties it has left the substantial minority of about 500 000, or over one-third of the entire population, who proclaim themselves as Irish rather than British (Table 3). In the neighbouring Irish Republic almost the entire population views the Nationalist and Catholic minority in the North as an unredeemed remnant of the Irish national movement which must eventually be politically reunited with the rest of Ireland. The one million Protestants are also viewed as Irishmen whose true interests also lie in an Irish Republic, and the persistence of British political authority is regarded as a characteristic attempt to perpetuate Britain's colonial past.

Clearly this outlook is totally at variance with that of the one million Protestants in Northern Ireland. They view themselves as being British and see the persistence of British political authority in the north-east as the continuing guarantee of their civic and political rights. Unification with the Irish Republic is therefore regarded as something totally out of the question, to be resisted by force of arms if necessary. Consequently, the Catholic minority in Northern Ireland is seen as a community of doubtful reliability whose basic loyalties are to a foreign country.

Attempted solutions

The basic nature of political life in Northern Ireland is so different from that in Great Britain that entirely different responses and solutions have been forthcoming. Instead of the situation in Britain where the two main parties alternate in office, manoeuvre for the 'middle ground' in politics, and seek to govern on the basis of consensus and compromise, Northern Ireland's has been a situation where one party has been in power since the 1920s and has sought to rule largely in the interests of its supporters alone. Conversely, the minority parties have been in perpetual opposition and their attitudes have varied from total boycott of all political life through protesting participation to Civil Rights agitation. In addition, throughout the history of Northern Ireland there have been small groups of people who have sought at various periods to advance their political ideals by military action.

For almost a decade after the partition of Ireland in 1920 the response of the Catholic community was total withdrawal and boycott of all forms of public life and service in Northern Ireland. Consequently, they refused to serve on public committees and authorities such as Boards of Guardians and Hospital and Education Committees. When elected to public office they refused to attend meetings or to participate in legislative procedures. Thus seats won by Nationalists at elections to local councils, the regional Parliament at Stormont and the British Parliament in London were not taken up. To become a full member of such bodies an Oath of Allegiance to the British Sovereign was required and many felt unable, as Irishmen, to take this. Moreover, to participate in the government and administration of Northern Ireland could be construed as *de facto* recognition and approval of Partition.

TABLE 3

Northern Ireland : Religious profession, 1961

	Total persons	Roman Catholic		Protestant		Others and not stated	
		total	per cent	total	per cent	total	per cent
Northern Ireland	1 425 042	497 547	34·9	829 778	58·2	97 717	6·9
Antrim	273 905	66 929	24·4	185 688	67·8	21 288	7·8
Armagh	117 594	55 617	47·3	55 972	47·6	6005	5·1
Down	266 939	76 263	28·6	168 659	63·2	22 017	8·2
Fermanagh	51 531	27 422	53·2	22 627	43·9	1482	2·9
Londonderry	111 536	47 509	42·6	58 861	52·8	5166	4·6
Tyrone	133 919	73 398	54·8	56 547	42·2	3974	3·0
Belfast C.B.	415 856	114 336	27·5	265 407	63·8	36 113	8·7
Londonderry, C.B.	53 762	36 073	67·1	16 017	29·8	1672	3·1

The strongly Protestant and pro-Union nature of the Unionist Party was in itself a considerable obstacle to Catholic membership, but this effect was further increased by an endemic tendency to mix simple anti-Catholicism with opposition to Irish Nationalism. The tendency was increased by the Unionist Party's link with the Orange Order. This Protestant organization was founded in Armagh in 1795. It has always been strongly opposed to Irish Nationalist aspirations and first developed an institutional link with the Unionist Party in 1909. Later the link became formalized and the Order nominates 122 of the 712 delegates to the Unionist Council, one of the most significant governing bodies within the party. However, its influence goes far beyond this formal association. Membership of the Order was for many years a prerequisite of nomination for a Unionist seat at Stormont or Westminster and also for membership of the Northern Ireland Cabinet. When added to the basically Protestant nature of the Unionist Party in general, the effect was strongly to rule out Catholic membership of the party.

The Protestant and Unionist response to lack of Catholic participation was to meet non-cooperation with total exclusion, and attempts were made to exclude Roman Catholics from positions of power and influence at various levels. This was largely done by manipulation of certain aspects of local government, particularly in those areas where Catholics were in a local majority. The local authority franchise in Northern Ireland remained a ratepayers' franchise until 1969, even though this was abolished in the rest of the United Kingdom in 1948. It was widely believed that it was retained to give the Unionists control over certain Catholic areas. In such districts Catholics had a majority of those aged 21 and over. However, Unionists had a majority of rate-payers, and the ratepayer franchise thus ensured that they would retain control of the council. In other areas where Catholics were locally dominant it now seems clear that the boundaries of local electoral areas were 'gerrymandered', or drawn with the deliberate intention of favouring the Unionists. Finally, when it became necessary to allocate local authority employment and housing, it also seems quite clear that Unionist councils favoured those who shared their particular sectarian outlook. Since councils were elected by ratepayer franchise, this could be a useful way of maintaining and strengthening the pattern of one's electoral support.

The period of Catholic and Nationalist boycott and non-cooperation lasted until the late 1920s and early 1930s. After that, Nationalists who secured election to public bodies and Parliament began to attend and take up their duties in increasing numbers. Even then, however, they tended to do so more as protesting representatives rather than as a potential alternative ruling group. They did not accept the status of Official Opposition at Stormont until 1965. Only at local government level were Catholics in sufficient strength in some areas of southern and western Ulster to gain control of local authorities, and there are indications that they pursued policies of discrimination in allocation of housing and employment as eagerly as the Unionists elsewhere.

Such a situation is clearly tense, unhappy, and basically immoral but over the years it seemed as if some sort of *modus vivendi* was emerging. The more elderly traditionally minded sections of the Catholic population tended to accept their role in the political system of Northern Ireland. While they may basically have hoped and wished for the unification of the six northern counties with the Irish Republic, they also operated the existing institutions because they gave opportunities for the airing of grievances and opinions. Moreover, as pointed out, there were opportunities for Catholic control of some councils and the services they provided. Even in those cases where Unionists were in control, and housing and employment were in their hands, the anti-Partition voice could still be heard.

It is doubtful if such arrangements could have persisted, however, and in the early 1960s impatient, younger elements in the Catholic community became dissatisfied with what they regarded as the Nationalist Party's passive acceptance of the Unionist hegemony. In 1967 and 1968 a series of Civil Rights demonstrations were organized in a campaign against religious discrimination in allocation of council employment and housing and in favour of universal franchise in local elections. Unfortunately these campaigns aroused traditional Protestant fears of Catholic aspirations for a United Ireland. Consequently tension rose rapidly and in the last months of 1968 and throughout 1969 there were frequent clashes between Protestants and Catholics, particularly in Belfast. The resources of the Royal Ulster Constabulary were soon exhausted as they attempted to separate the two groups, especially in Londonderry, and in August 1969 British troops were deployed.

The communal riots in this latter month also saw the reactivation of another group with a distinctively military solution to the problems of Northern Ireland, namely the I.R.A. The

Support for the Irish Republican movement is strong in the Catholic districts of Belfast. Parades are held each Easter to commemorate the 1916 Rising in Dublin

original Irish Republican Army had been involved in the Dublin Easter Rising of 1916 and the subsequent guerilla wars of 1918–21 against the British forces. It had split in 1922 over the peace settlement with Great Britain and a notable faction led by Eamon De Valera had waged an unsuccessful civil war for a period. In 1926 those opposed to this settlement decided to reorganize themselves as a Republican political party and participate fully in the political life of the new Irish State. Once again however the Republican

movement split, because a large group did not approve of this decision being taken. This group then took upon themselves the name and the mantle of the I.R.A., and now viewed both Northern Ireland and the Southern Irish Free State as illegitimate political entities to be destroyed by force if necessary. During the 1920s they had waged a campaign of sabotage and guerilla warfare against Northern Ireland but this was called off in the early 1930s from lack of success. It revived somewhat in the early

27

months of World War II in the hope of capitalizing on British preoccupation elsewhere and German aid, but once again was unsuccessful. The same was true of a campaign conducted between 1955 and 1962, mostly comprising raids on police and customs posts in border areas. In the following years the remnants of the I.R.A. appear to have become increasingly committed to conventional party politics and they eventually adopted many left-wing outlooks on social and economic issues in all parts of Ireland. During the communal riots in Belfast in August 1969 it was claimed by some elements in the organization that this pre-occupation with theoretical Marxism and policy-making was to blame for the heavy loss of life and property in the Catholic districts. Consequently the I.R.A. split into an 'Official' group still retaining the Marxist and political orientation developed in the mid-1960s and a 'Provisional' wing aiming at the defence of Catholic areas and the unification of Ireland by the historic means of guerilla warfare.

The Provisional I.R.A. made the Catholic areas of Belfast its bases and from there organized a steadily mounting campaign of sniping at security forces and bombing of commercial premises in the city centre. By August 1971 this had reached such a crescendo that internment of suspected I.R.A. members without trial was introduced. While considerable amounts of arms, explosives, and information were acquired during the subsequent arrests and interrogations, the Catholic community was totally alienated from the British Army and support for the Provisional I.R.A. increased considerably. Within a few months the level of bombings and shootings had far surpassed its previous level. The situation was made even more desperate by the fact that all the Opposition members with one exception boycotted Stormont and called on all Catholics to withdraw from public life until internment ended. The situation was made worse when security forces shot dead thirteen Catholic demonstrators in Londonderry's Bogside in January, 1972.

Faced with a political deadlock plus a rapidly worsening military situation, the British Government decided that a series of new approaches must be attempted to isolate the I.R.A. from the Catholic community and persuade the Opposition to re-enter the political arena. In March 1972 it was proposed to the Northern Ireland Government that internment should be phased out and responsibility for security transferred to London. This last they refused to accept. On 30 March 1972, the Stormont Parliament was prorogued for a year and an entirely new post of Secretary of State for Northern Ireland was created.

The basic task of the new Secretary was formidable: to isolate the I.R.A. from the Catholic community and defeat them, to end the Opposition boycott of all forms of political life, and to restructure the institutions of Northern Ireland to provide opportunities for the full participation and fair treatment of all groups. Internment was gradually reduced after March 1972 and some of the Opposition groups were persuaded to join with the Unionists in a conference in August the same year. However, the Secretary of State had very little room for political manoeuvre because, as pointed out earlier, in Northern Ireland the aspirations of each community are the anathema of the other. It was eventually proposed that Stormont should be replaced by an Assembly with powers over most internal affairs except security. The Assembly was to consist of 78 members elected by a proportional representation system from multi-member constituencies. It was suggested that the exercise of power should be shared between representatives of the two communities. The first elections were held in June 1973.

4 The Regional Problem

Introduction

Thus far attention has been concentrated on the economic and political problems of Northern Ireland in such a way as to suggest that they are similar in nature and intensity throughout the entire six constituent counties. Despite the relatively small size of the province there are in fact considerable internal variations in the severity and interrelationships of the problems encountered.

The basic regional divide in Northern Ireland is between the eastern areas comprising most of counties Down, Antrim, and north Armagh, and the western counties of Fermanagh, Tyrone, parts of Londonderry, south Armagh, and south Down. The western areas tend to have a markedly agricultural and rural way of life (Table 4). Here, too, very few new economic activities have been established and unemployment has always been much higher than in the east. The eastern counties by contrast have a high level of non-agricultural employment and urban-dwelling; unemployment has always been much lower than the

Northern Ireland average and the small agricultural sector is modern and commercialized.

There are also considerable contrasts in political life and problems. The west is much more strongly Roman Catholic and Irish Nationalist or Republican and in counties Fermanagh and Tyrone and parts of Londonderry, south Armagh, and south Down they outnumber the Protestants (Fig. 5). Consequently the struggle for power at the local level has often been particularly factious and bitter. In the east the economic and political problems are a heritage of the Industrial Revolution. Whilst the Protestant communities in these areas are in an overwhelming majority, there are small Catholic communities in all the large urban centres, particularly in west Belfast, who were originally attracted by the economic opportunities of the nineteenth century. Their high degree of residential segregation resulting from past outbreaks of communal rioting has created ideal enclaves for support of the urban guerilla warfare which broke out in 1970.

TABLE 4

Northern Ireland : Population centres of 5000 and over in 1971

Centre	Population	Centre	Population
County Boroughs		**Co. Armagh**	
Belfast	360 150	Armagh U.D.	12 297
Londonderry	51 850	Craigavon U.D.	12 594
		Lurgan M.B.	24 055
Co. Antrim		Portadown M.B.	21 906
Antrim	7 320		
Ballyclare U.D.	5144	**Co. Fermanagh**	
Ballymena M.B.	16 487	—	—
Carrickfergus M.B.	15 162		
Larne M.B.	18 242	**Co. Tyrone**	
Lisburn M.B.	27 405	Cookstown U.D.	6673
Newtownabbey U.D.	57 908	Dungannon U.D.	7535
		Armagh U.D.	11 953
Co. Down		Strabane U.D.	9325
Banbridge U.D.	6864		
Bangor M.B.	35 178	**Co. Londonderry**	
Comber	5193	Coleraine M.B.	14 871
Downpatrick U.D.	7403	Limavady M.B.	5555
Holywood U.D.	7980		
Newry U.D.	11 393		
Newtownards M.B.	15 387		

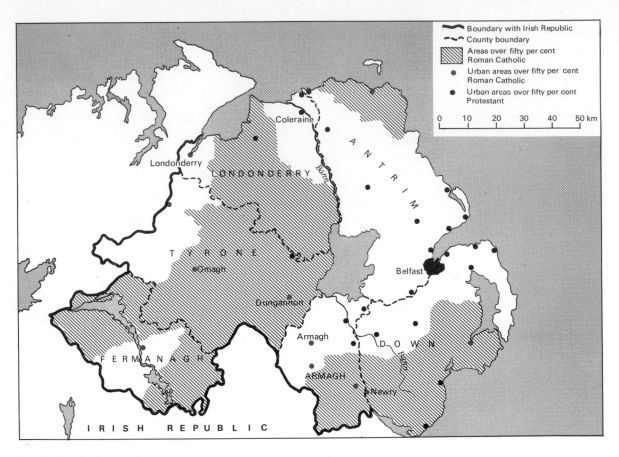

Legend:
- Boundary with Irish Republic
- County boundary
- Areas over fifty per cent Roman Catholic
- Urban areas over fifty per cent Roman Catholic
- Urban areas over fifty per cent Protestant

0 10 20 30 40 50 km

Coleraine

A N T R I M

Londonderry

L O N D O N D E R R Y

Bann

T Y R O N E

Omagh

Belfast

Dungannon

Armagh

D O W N

Bann

F E R M A N A G H

A R M A G H

Newry

I R I S H   R E P U B L I C

Fig. 5. Distribution of religious groups

The western areas
The nature of the problem

The western areas of Northern Ireland are those districts in which the agricultural and rural nature once characteristic of the entire six counties has persisted longest. In general, just over 13 per cent of the labour force of the Province of Northern Ireland is still employed in agriculture. In counties Londonderry, Tyrone, and Fermanagh, however, the level is higher, reaching 38 per cent in county Fermanagh. Moreover, the form of agriculture in these areas tends to be less sophisticated than elsewhere. It is in the remoter areas of these counties that one still encounters farmhouses without electricity, large numbers of small uneconomic holdings and a notably high level of employment of family labour. This last means that underemployment is chronic on the farms of the western counties since sons and daughters tend to stay and to be retained on the farm for sentimental and family reasons even when the holding is not large enough to justify their remaining on economic grounds alone.

However, as an employer of labour, agriculture is contracting in the western and southern areas as elsewhere. Unfortunately, there are relatively few alternative occupations available in these districts. The economic base is remarkably narrow and the influx of new employment opportunities has been small. One of the results of this is that these remote western and southern districts usually have the highest unemployment percentage of any part of Northern Ireland. Thus in 1971 statistics showed an overall figure of 8·1 per cent unemployed for the entire six counties, but Londonderry City and County together with counties Armagh, Tyrone, and Fermanagh were all well above this level—for Strabane and district it was 16·7 per cent.

It is hardly surprising, therefore, that these areas have a high rate of emigration, either to urban areas or overseas to Great Britain, and since there are very few economic openings in local urban centres any emigration must be a relatively long distance affair to urban centres in the eastern part of the Province or to Great

Glenelly Valley, Co. Tyrone. High density of rural settlement and large number of small fields are a notable problem in the western areas of Northern Ireland

Britain. This is a notable factor in explaining the reluctance of some people to move at all.

Such problems are not of course unique to Northern Ireland. They can be closely duplicated in any rural areas remote from large population centres, such as Central Wales, the Scottish Highlands, the Massif Central of France, and the Alps of Central Europe. In Northern Ireland, however, they are further complicated by the question of political nationalism. As one proceeds west and south from Belfast the percentage of pro-Unionists declines while that of Irish Nationalists and Republicans increases. This relationship holds true to the point where Catholics are in an actual majority in counties Fermanagh and Tyrone and in some parts of other counties such as Londonderry City, Ballycastle and north Antrim, Armagh City and south-east Armagh, Downpatrick, Newry, and south Down (Fig. 5). These are the areas which caused considerable dispute in the years before Partition in 1920 when the Nationalists and Republicans bitterly contested their loss and the Unionists insisted on their inclusion within Northern Ireland to create a viable political unit. These basic conflicts have persisted in these areas and in view of the fine balance of populations and loyalties, it is hardly surprising that the local power struggles have been bitter and long-lasting.

Causes of the problem

One of the basic reasons for the distribution of religious and political groups, urban living, and industrialization is the factor of distance from the original entry points of colonization and settlement. It is possible to view these spatial distributions within the framework of a 'distance decay' model describing the degree of adoption of a series of innovations. The innovations in question are Protestanism and urban living, as originally introduced in the early seventeenth century by the English and Scots planters. The original entry points were on the eastern coasts of Ulster, particularly through south Antrim and north Down and the Lagan Valley. As the settlers

31

proceeded south and westwards the factor of 'spatial friction' came into play. Increasing distance from the original source of the innovations and the initial zone of entry led to a progressive falling away in numbers, until over large areas of what later became Fermanagh, Tyrone, and Londonderry the native Irish Catholic population and way of life were relatively undisturbed and the Protestant Planters were in a localized minority. The towns established by the Planters operated for a long time as secondary transmitters of these innovations and this is particularly true of Londonderry. The process of industrialization, which struck deepest roots in the eastern part of the Province, may be viewed within broadly the same model. It was with industrialization that the character of many of the urban centres in Ulster changed dramatically. It will be recalled that they were originally Planter foundations with a population of Protestant citizens intended to garrison, civilize, and provide services for surrounding rural areas. With the passage of time the greater economic opportunities of these urban areas began to attract immigrants from the rural districts. In the western parts of the province, where Catholics often comprised a majority of the local population, migration eventually changed the character of the urban populations and towns such as Londonderry, Amagh, Enniskillen, and Newry acquired a Catholic majority. The relatively large urban centres of the east such as Lurgan, Lisburn, and Belfast shared in the process of migration and though they remained strongly Protestant they acquired small Catholic populations who came to live in distinctive sectors of the towns. The later developments of Irish Nationalism and Ulster Unionism took root in the Catholic and Protestant populations respectively and the spatial distribution of these attitudes may also be viewed as an indirect result of the workings of the 'distance decay' model.

If the original location of industrial development in the east of Ulster can be related to the operation of this model, then the contemporary lack of modern economic development in western Ulster can also be viewed as a result of it. The long-term build-up of urban centres, population, and economic activity in the eastern areas has given them considerable advantage in the attraction of new industrial activity. There a considerable skilled labour pool and potential market are already in existence. The infrastructure of communications, services, and social opportunities is also relatively sophisticated. Moreover, this is the part of Northern Ireland closest to

Great Britain and Western Europe, the sources of many of the new economic undertakings and the eventual destination of many of their end products. The far western and southern areas by contrast suffer from the greater travel times, distances, and costs due to their relative location. Communications and service facilities are relatively poor and there are no really large urban centres. This last point is a decided disadvantage when efforts are being made to attract new industrial activity. Superficially, unemployment levels such as 13·3 per cent (Londonderry C.B., January 1972) suggest a large pool of surplus labour attractive to industrialists. In fact relatively small numbers of people are involved. In the Londonderry example, about 3000 people comprised the 13·3 per cent. This is approximately the workforce of one fairly large industrial establishment. In some of the smaller urban centres even lower totals are involved—a 10 per cent unemployment rate means 340 people available in Cookstown, 560 in Strabane. Unfortunately, these totals are too small to provide labour forces for the large industrial establishments characteristic of modern economic activity.

The nature and intensity of the political problems also alter in the western parts of the Province. These are the areas where the balance of population between Protestants and Catholics is very fine—or else the Catholics have an outright majority—hence many Protestants fear that they are well on the way to seeing their absorption into a Catholic dominated State. Since these are the parts of Northern Ireland closest to the Irish Republic, there is much to reinforce this fear. It has been further driven home by the activities of the I.R.A. which used the nearby Republic as a base to mount a guerilla warfare campaign against security forces and installations in the border areas between 1955 and 1961, and during the early 1970s.

The Protestant and Unionist populations of western and southern Ulster thus acquired a particularly intransigent outlook because of their numerical and spatial position. This frequently resulted in manipulation of local government boundaries, services, and employment and strong support for the Orange Order and the 'B' Special Constabulary. The Catholic response was particularly bitter. This was reflected in electoral support for extreme Republican candidates, particularly at Westminster elections, when the seats of Mid-Ulster and Fermanagh/South Tyrone were frequently won by Sinn Fein, the political arm of the I.R.A. In the mid-1960s it was in these areas that the Civil Rights Association found strong support and organized campaigns and demonstrations in centres such as Coalisland and Dungannon. It is not without significance, therefore, that the troubles of the late 1960s followed on from a Civil Rights demonstration in Londonderry on 5 October 1968.

Attempted solutions

For a long period no solutions at all were advanced for the economic and political problems of the remoter areas of western and southern Ulster. This may have been due to the fact that knowledge of their nature and intensity was not widespread. In economic affairs in particular it is also possible that elements of *laissez-faire* doctrine encouraged the belief that nothing could or should be done to aid the western areas.

Inevitably, in view of the nature of Northern Ireland's political problems, there were suspicions that far from trying to attract industry to these remote areas, the Unionist Government at Stormont was actively persuading it to go elsewhere simply because these areas were largely Catholic. In the 1960s there was a similar suspicion amongst the Protestants of the west. Perhaps they recalled the manner in which the Protestant communities of the rest of Ireland and particularly those of Donegal, Cavan, and Monaghan had been regarded as expendable at the Partition of 1920 and they feared a similar decision on economic development had been taken 40 years later. It must be said, however, that there is no firm evidence of such an intentional policy of large-scale areal discrimination. It seems much more likely that the reasons of location, population size, and infrastructure already discussed comprise the true explanation. Nonetheless, given the mutual incomprehension and mistrust between the two communities of Northern Ireland it is virtually impossible to allay such suspicions.

With the passage of time there came an increasing official awareness of the needs and potentialities of the remoter parts of the Province. A programme of advance factory construction was begun whereby the Ministry of Commerce built standard factories in certain areas before they actually had tenants for them. The hope was that the existence of such structures would attract firms looking for space for expansion who could then occupy them within a relatively short time, not having to wait for them to be built. There were a few limited successes, most notably the decision of a synthetic fibres knitting plant to transfer all their operations from England to an advance factory in Strabane. In general,

however, the relative deprivation of the remoter areas persisted.

In 1964 the Northern Ireland Government launched a multi-purpose roads programme. One of its aims was the continuation and expansion of the traditional practice of relieving local unemployment by public works, particularly road construction and improvement. A further motive was to overcome problems of relative location. It was hoped that the improvement of roads would reduce travel times and render various parts of Northern Ireland more accessible, not least the remote southern and western districts. The emphasis on speedy modern travel was exemplified by the decision to spend over one-third (£32 million) of the total estimates on roads of motorway standard. Total expenditure was later reduced from £66 million to £51 million because of other claims on capital resources, but the motorway construction scheme was retained, though in a rephased form. The first major section to be completed was significantly from Belfast up the Lagan Valley past Craigavon to Dungannon. The second was planned to connect Belfast to Ballymena via Antrim and though progress suffered considerably from the necessary reallocation of resources and rephasing of the construction programme, it was almost completed by early 1973.

A long-term reappraisal of the role of Northern Ireland's railways accompanied and partly explained the programme of road construction. A considerable reduction of the railway network occurred in the early 1960s and a decade later the closure of the line from Ballymena to Londonderry was also under serious consideration. The economic case for such reappraisal was strong. Virtually none of the railway lines in Northern Ireland were a viable economic proposition. The consultants engaged on the 1970–5 Development Programme commented: 'Their abolition would do no more than add a single year's traffic growth to a road system which at present would be well able to accommodate it.'. However, it was recognized that at the same time uneconomic railway lines were likely to be retained '. . . mainly for social and political reasons'. The result is that the Ballymena–Londonderry line was reprieved and in general terms Northern Ireland has a more extensive rail network and a road network of greater density and higher standard than present or foreseeable future traffic would merit. Whether or not this succeeds in attracting new economic undertakings, particularly to the remoter areas, remains to be seen.

33

Adria Knitting Mills, Strabane, Co. Tyrone. This synthetic fibre plant, transferred *en bloc* from Great Britain, is probably the most successful of the advance factories in the west of Northern Ireland

One of the drawbacks about such schemes as advance factories and communications improvements is their uncoordinated and piecemeal nature. Advance factories were not necessarily located close to motorways or improved standard roads: such motorways were not always planned in relation to the most favourable centres of future economic development. Instead the tendency was to locate advance factories and improve roads in areas where unemployment was particularly high. The criteria utilized were social and curative rather than economic and preventative. Unfortunately most of the urban structure of the western areas is very basic (Table 4) and significant parts of the service infrastructure are deficient; advance factories are provided and local communications improved only haphazardly; total populations are small and social opportunities limited.

The concept of the growth centre was adopted to overcome these disadvantages. The idea behind this approach is to concentrate future development on those existing local centres of population and economic development which offer the best prospects for future growth. Consequently, the local and regional communications of a centre are improved; nearby sites for factory development are purchased, cleared, and provided with basic amenities and possibly advance factories; housing is provided for shop-floor, administrative, and management workers; and sections of the town may be cleared and redeveloped to modernize and increase retail and service outlets and to provide a more pleasant environment. Such an approach has many advantages for a small area with limited resources as is Nothern Ireland.

West of the river Bann six urban centres have been designated as 'key centres' for concentration of economic growth (Fig. 6). Development plans have been produced for these towns and their surrounding areas and considerable improvements in both infrastructure and environment are under way. To varying extents the Ministry of Commerce has acquired and prepared industrial sites; access roads and services are being laid out, local communications improved, water and sewage capacities extended, and town centres cleared, redeveloped, and expanded to serve the greater demands from the population influx expected; large areas of new housing are also being built to accommodate people displaced by clearance and also to house the anticipated new residents.

Of all the urban centres in the west, Londonderry has received most attention. Here economic and social problems have been particularly acute. The natural increase rate of population has long been the greatest of any city in the United Kingdom; throughout the 1960s unemployment was never below the 10 per cent level; amongst men it was usually over 18 per cent. Sentimental and political considerations also gave it a prominent place in Ulster history and politics and generated much unsavoury publicity. Despite these drawbacks the site and surrounding area did manage to attract significant new manufacturing activities during the 1960s. In 1968 a firm of planning consultants produced the Londonderry Area Plan for the period 1968–81 which set a number of targets for growth and suggested appropriate improvements in services and communications. It was thought that 6000 more manufacturing jobs would be needed by 1981. To serve the expanded traffic volume it was recommended that considerable improvements

to the harbour, quays, and access roads were necessary. It was further considered that the total population would be 75 000 to 80 000 by 1981. To provide for this total it was recommended that five nearby villages should be expanded, 9600 new dwellings provided, the city's central shopping area made a more specialized traffic-free zone, and additional neighbourhood facilities made available in two parts of the city. Before these recommendations could find concrete expression they were overtaken by the rapidly deteriorating political situation. One of the consequences of this was the designation of a Development Commission with responsibility for both Londonderry County Borough and the nearby Rural District. Following its appointment in February 1969 this body proceeded to discharge its duties and implement the consultants' recommendations with considerable speed and skill. Unfortunately, the recent economic progress of Londonderry has been thrown into doubt by political insecurity.

The insecure numerical and spatial position of the Protestants in western areas meant that the

Fig. 6. Designated growth areas

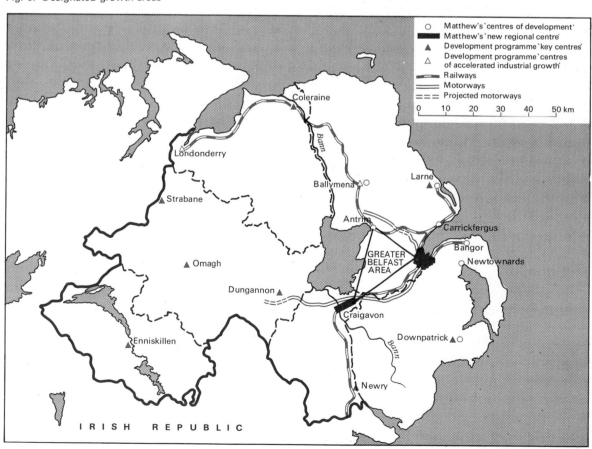

struggle for political power was often particularly bitter. Convincing allegations of gerrymandering to the advantage of the Unionists were made of Armagh, Dungannon, County Fermanagh, Omagh, and above all, Londonderry. Here in the late 1960s the ratepayer franchise produced an electorate of approximately 7900 Protestants and 10 000 Catholics. In view of the rigidly sectarian lines of Northern Irish voting an anti-Partition controlled council would have appeared inevitable. However, for most of the present century the city has been Unionist controlled. In the local government elections of 1967, 14 429 anti-Partition votes produced 8 councillors, while 8781 Unionist votes produced 12 councillors and thus a controlling majority. This was achieved by the careful creation of three wards in the city. The boundaries were drawn in such a way that almost three-quarters of the Catholic electors were in South Ward, which thus had a total electorate almost four times greater than the others. The remaining two wards were both strongly Protestant. No really satisfactory explanation was ever advanced for the considerable variations in size of ward populations and electorates and the strange results. The outcome, however, was clear, namely a marked Unionist minority of votes was changed into a majority of seats and overall political control of a strongly Catholic and anti-Partition city.

Apart from the general Protestant apprehensions about the ultimate loyalties and intentions of the Catholic population—considerably sharpened by the very fine balance of the population in these western areas—there were additional motives for such practices. One was largely historic and emotional. Many of the urban centres of western Ulster have been closely associated with dates and events significant for the Protestant community and they were unwilling to see their opponents in effective control of their local council, regardless of their numbers. Londonderry was a prime example of this. It was originally a Planter town whose name recalls its early associations with the London merchant companies who financed much of its founding. In 1689 when nearly all of Ireland rose to support James II's attempt to regain his throne, Londonderry held out for William III. It endured a grim siege of 15 weeks, relieved only when a number of food ships forced the passage of the River Foyle. The defence became legendary in Ulster Protestant history as a symbol of grim and ultimately successful struggle against Catholic Irish aspirations and has been immortalized in Orange banners, slogans, and marching songs.

The Protestant Apprentice Boys Clubs in particular preserve these memories. Clearly, therefore, Londonderry means much to Ulster Protestants and Unionists.

However, there was more than simple emotion and historical association behind gerrymandering. In Northern Ireland control of local authorities meant the ability to distribute council housing and to a lesser extent employment to one's own supporters. In view of this closely interrelated situation of economic deprivation and political malpractice, it is hardly surprising that the early Civil Rights campaign concentrated much of its attention on local government grievances in western Ulster. One of its first public protests was against dubious decisions on house allocation by Dungannon Rural District; its first large demonstration was in the town of Dungannon in August 1968 and the troubles of the late 1960s and early 1970s stemmed from the Londonderry demonstration on 5 October 1968.

The eastern areas

The nature of the problem

A significant proportion of the residential area of Belfast is composed of dwellings almost a century old. These usually take the form of brick-built terrace houses, often back-to-back with a narrow alley-way between, an exterior lavatory and originally without a bathroom or hot water. Despite the improvements made by successive generations of occupiers there are still large areas of west Belfast and districts of north and east Belfast close to the city centre where households must live in accommodation which by contemporary criteria is decidedly sub-standard.

In the early 1960s it was estimated that the city needed 58 700 new houses. Of this total, about 18 000 were replacements for dwellings declared totally unfit for human occupation. Several thousand were to replace prefabricated dwellings originally built to house families made homeless by the air raids of 1941. The balance consisted of the normal waiting list, which is added to each year by the substantial natural increase in population. The situation was further aggravated by the widely acknowledged fact that in Belfast—as one eminent consultant put it—'housing by the public authority has been minimal'. From 1945 until the late 1960s Belfast Corporation built new houses at the rate of less than 300 each year. As early as 1960 the situation had become so serious that the Northern Ireland Ministry of Health and Local Government expressed concern in a memorandum and gave a

Clearance and redevelopment of a nineteenth century working-class area in West Belfast. The high density of housing and the proximity to the factories is characteristic of the period

suggested target of 2000 public authority houses each year for the next decade as the minimum necessary.

A further complication arose from the fact that in and around the city in the early 1960s there were only building sites for a further 22 350 dwellings thus leaving space for 36 350 more to be found. The most natural places to find these sites were in nearby small towns, villages, and rural areas. However, a good deal of private development of this type had already taken place over the years. In the early 1960s projections based on such trends suggested that if they continued unchecked then by 1981 the Greater Belfast Area would have a total population of at least 700 000.

Considerable thought was devoted to the likely consequences of these developments. Clearly it would mean that the predominance of the east and in particular of the Belfast region would be considerably reinforced and the remote western and southern parts of the Province would be relatively worse off. There would also be a continuous sprawl of residential and industrial areas along both shores of Belfast Lough and the Lagan Valley. As a result the surrounding rural areas would suffer severely. Considerable tracts of first class agricultural land would be lost. Possibly even more disastrous in the long run would be the destruction of the amenity value of tracts of upland and coastal scenery in the Lagan Valley, the Holywood Hills, and the shores of Belfast Lough, Strangford Lough, and Lough Neagh.

Furthermore, it seemed highly likely that the inner areas of Belfast itself would suffer considerably from unchecked economic and population growth. Like most major British cities, the downtown areas of Belfast have a road system inherited from past decades when road transport was much simpler in form and smaller in volume. The large-scale growth and development of wheeled traffic and the decline of the railways put a considerable strain on the city's road system and produced the familiar problems of traffic congestion, pollution, noise, and accidents. Further increase in population and economic activity would inevitably add to the problems of circulation of people, goods, and animals.

In 1963 Sir Robert Matthew was engaged to investigate and make recommendations on the Belfast region. His report suggested that many of the difficulties and trends then emerging could be attributed in part at least to the absence of proper planning. There had been no really adequate

and continuous planning survey of the Urban Area and what little work had been done was largely on an uncoordinated, piecemeal basis: indeed since the Second World War this was largely true of Northern Ireland as a whole. Unlike the situation in Great Britain, town planning was not a recognized or important function in the government of Northern Ireland. Certainly there was interest, initiative, and a certain amount of work being done in various departments, but it was being done in isolation and the end product was very often a less than optimal use of land.

This report proved to be one of the most influential documents ever produced on any aspect of development in Northern Ireland.

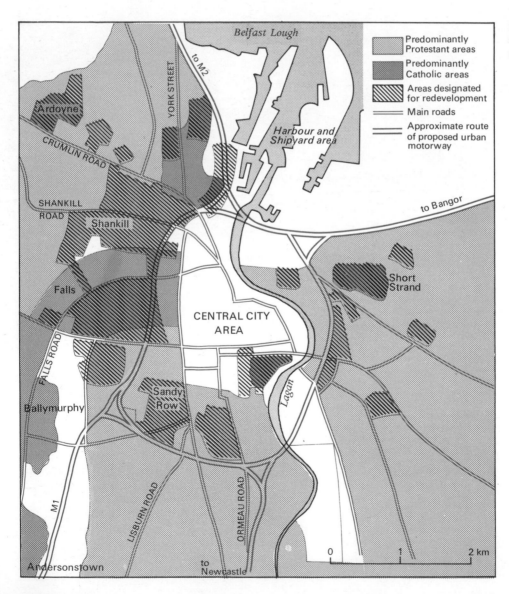

Fig. 7. Belfast: segregation and redevelopment

Predominantly Protestant areas
Predominantly Catholic areas
Areas designated for redevelopment
Main roads
Approximate route of proposed urban motorway

Belfast Lough

to M2
YORK STREET
Harbour and Shipyard area
Ardoyne
CRUMLIN ROAD
SHANKILL ROAD
Shankill
to Bangor
Falls
Short Strand
CENTRAL CITY AREA
FALLS ROAD
Lagan
Sandy Row
Ballymurphy
M1
LISBURN ROAD
ORMEAU ROAD
Andersonstown
to Newcastle

0   1   2 km

This triumphal arch in a Protestant district of East Belfast vividly expresses the pro-Unionist sentiment of the local community

Unfortunately, because of its terms of reference, it could not deal with what has proved to be one of the most intractable of all Belfast's problems, namely spatial segregation of the population on the basis of sectarian loyalties. In most studies of British cities it has been found that spatial segregation of residential areas is on the basis of social class, though there are also indications that ethnic origin has become important in recent years. In Belfast and most of the urban centres of Northern Ireland, however, sectarian political loyalty appears to be an equally significant determining principle (Fig. 7).

There are thus large areas of Belfast inhabited almost solely by Protestants or Catholics. There are four Catholic districts. The smallest and most isolated lies just east of the river Lagan which flows through the city. Two other small areas are in north Belfast, almost entirely surrounded by Protestant districts. The fourth and by far the largest Catholic district of all lies in the western and south-western sector of the city. Its apex is the earliest Roman Catholic church in Belfast just west of the city centre and it stretches away from this in a westerly and south-westerly direction along the line of the Falls Road, one of the main access routes. Each of these districts is almost totally Catholic and anti-Partition in outlook and each is surrounded by areas equally strongly Protestant and Unionist.

The character and intensity of the segregation may be gauged from study of Census returns and also by careful observation of the nature and type of slogans, street decorations, flags, and wall paintings with which each community embellishes its respective areas. Activities are as spatially segregated as residence. Each group holds processions and demonstrations on particular dates to commemorate significant events and the routes of these processions are normally confined to

39

their respective areas. However, activity segregation goes much further and deeper than this. Survey analysis has revealed that even the non-political activities of daily life are segregated. Journeys to work and shop are almost entirely confined to one's 'own' area, and a bus-stop on a route through the territory of the opposing side is avoided where possible, even though it may provide a shorter route. Journeys to school are also segregated because the Catholic community prefers separate education in Church schools. Partly as a result of this and partly because of the all-pervading nature of the political and sectarian cleavage in Northern Irish society, friendship and inter-marriage between individuals of differing religions and political outlooks are rare and consequently even social visiting is spatially segregated.

Despite the obvious drawbacks of such a pattern of social geography, there are also certain compensations. It has been a sad truism of life in Northern Ireland that 'mixed' residential areas have usually been the scene of severe communal conflict as a result of which the area in question is evacuated by one group and soon becomes entirely the preserve of another. Residential segregation may thus be viewed as a necessary, if unpleasant, way to preserve civic peace, and on these grounds the allocation of all houses in an estate to people of uniform sectarian outlook is quite understandable. Another compensating feature of life in these areas is their strong sense of community identity. Most of the Protestant districts support Orange lodges, often based on local churches. Since the disturbances of the late 1960s this community sentiment has been diverted into other channels. The I.R.A. has recruited heavily in the Catholic districts and for a period of almost two years down to mid-1972 the Catholic districts of Belfast and Londonderry were virtually I.R.A. dominated enclaves inside Northern Ireland. Early on in the crisis the Protestant areas organized local vigilante groups for the patrolling and protecting of their areas. As the crisis deepened, the activities of the I.R.A. became intensified and the Protestant districts began to organize themselves, first into Defence Committees and finally as local units of the Ulster Defence Association and various other groups.

Causes of the problem

As a result of the massive expansion of economic activity, the population of Belfast grew rapidly during the nineteenth century. In 1821 it had been just over 30 000; by 1871 it was 180 000 and by 1911 the total was 390 000. The attraction of Belfast for migrants was two-fold. Firstly, during most of the nineteenth century, and especially after the Famine of 1846–8, the Irish economy was undergoing a process of transformation. The almost universal system of peasant subsistence agriculture based largely on potato cultivation collapsed under the impact of potato blight. The immediate result was that thousands of people left the rural areas for the towns to seek relief, employment, or passages overseas. In subsequent years there was a change of emphasis in Irish agriculture from peasant subsistence to commercial pastoral farming. This involved extensive eviction of tenants and was much less labour intensive, with the result that many more people sought employment elsewhere. Inevitably they gravitated towards the urban areas, and in particular towards Belfast.

The attractions of the city were considerable because the industrial developments already outlined inevitably meant that a large number of economic openings were available. Despite the occasional downward fluctuations of economic activity, the overall picture in the city during the nineteenth century was one of steadily growing and diversifying opportunities which were particularly attractive against a background of recession and contraction in the rural economy.

To accommodate the influx, housing had to be built as rapidly and economically as possible. Local authority bye-laws setting minimum standards for size and amenities had been enacted, particularly in 1857 and 1878. Consequently, the great expansion of house-building in the second half of the nineteenth century produced the large areas of brick-built terraces conforming to these regulations which characterize much of working-class Belfast. It has been pointed out that since the city experienced its maximum period of industrial and population expansion later than most British towns, conditions and housing standards may have been rather better. By modern standards, however, the houses erected during this phase of expansion are grossly inadequate. The dimensions of the problem may be gauged from the fact that as late as the mid-1960s virtually every house built to the 1857 bye-law standards was still occupied. By this time standards of public authority housing and social expectations had risen considerably and the houses in question had begun to deteriorate after several generations of occupation. In much of their outward physical appearance the working-class areas of Belfast which date from this period, are noted more for monotonous uniformity than aesthetic appeal.

There is some evidence that urban residential segregation was known in Plantation times. Thus in early maps and documents there are indications of distinct 'Irish Quarters', often outside the city walls. However, the phenomenon seems to have been short-lived, because by the mid-eighteenth century the returns of Belfast's population were recording that about 7 per cent of the inhabitants *within* the town were Irish Roman Catholics. It seems likely that any spatial segregation which was present at this period was simply due to the persistence of the districts created by the original Plantation.

Community relations at this point were reasonably harmonious, thanks to the political inertness and lack of leadership of the Catholic community, and the fact that Protestant Dissenters also suffered from legal disabilities created a certain identity of interest.

Then, in the early nineteenth century, the situation began to deteriorate, due to the rapidly accelerating divergence of political outlook and loyalties. In the urban centres, and above all in Belfast, an almost equally significant factor which provoked Protestant apprehensions was the rapid growth of the Catholic community. In Belfast in 1776 it was probably about 8·4 per cent of the total, but by 1834 it had almost quadrupled to 32·4 per cent and the return for 1861 was 34·1 per cent. This phenomenal growth was largely a response to the rapid changes in the relative economic attractiveness of Belfast and the rural areas. That the Catholic element should be particularly large was due to two factors. First, the Famine and subsequent changes in agricultural structure did not hit the nearby Protestant districts in Antrim, Down, and Armagh as hard as elsewhere because there the cultivation of flax and working of linen yarn and cloth was a widespread supplementary source of income. In Ulster the greatest impact was felt in the more outlying counties of Donegal, Cavan, Monaghan, Tyrone, and Fermanagh, where this extra element was less significant in the rural economy. Inhabitants of these areas thus had a stronger motive for movement and since these were strongly Catholic districts, the large Catholic element in the migration resulted. It was further increased by the recently completed railway system and an improved network of roads which facilitated population movement not only from Ulster but from almost everywhere in Ireland.

As the Roman Catholic migrants entered the city the areas they chose for residence were determined by several factors. There were three main passenger rail terminals in Belfast and few of the newly arrived immigrants had the desire, knowledge, or finance to search for living quarters far from their point of arrival. In most cases they had come in search of work and the attraction of the districts around the railway terminals was increased by their proximity to textile and tobacco mills, chemical and engineering works, the shipyards and docks. The Catholic migrants inevitably came into competition for accommodation and employment with Protestant migrants and moreover their constantly growing numbers seriously alarmed the Protestant residents of Belfast. In these circumstances the final factor of community conflict was almost inevitable. Groups of like-minded people inevitably congregate for purposes of mutual protection. In the case of the Catholics the four districts noted earlier (page 39) were the result. The location of a parish church within these Catholic districts is both effect and cause of spatial concentration of Catholics. Each of the main districts has a church and while a certain basic population must clearly be resident in an area to make this a necessary and viable proposition, its construction tends to confirm and perpetuate the outlook of the district concerned. The appearance of residences and facilities for teaching, charitable, and contemplative orders, the building of church schools and organization of parish-based social and sporting clubs has a similar effect.

Attempted solutions

The problems of the eastern districts of Northern Ireland have received more public attention than those of the west because these are the areas where the vast majority of the population and most of the economic activity are found. Significantly, the problems of segregation have remained virtually untouched.

The aim of the strategy tackling the problems of the Belfast region has been described as '. . . simultaneously to de-magnetize the centre, and re-invigorate the many attractive small towns in the region.'. To this end Sir Robert Matthew, the planning consultant, produced a detailed regional plan in 1963. It was decided to limit the future development of the Belfast area so that by 1981 the total population would be only 600 000, an increase of nearly 40 000 from 1963. To this end it was recommended that a 'stopline' should be delimited beyond which the future growth and development of the area should not encroach.

Recently completed public authority housing on the outskirts of Belfast, with emphasis on low density, spacious layout and greenery

Two developments were proposed to deal with the surplus of 100 000 people which migration and natural increase would otherwise concentrate in the Belfast area. The first was the creation of a new regional centre to act as a counter-magnet. It was proposed that this should be located south of Lough Neagh and should be based on the existing centres of Lurgan and Portadown. In 1962 their combined population was approximately 36 000. Under the regional plan it was proposed that this should reach 100 000 by 1981. It was suggested that by taking advantage of its location in relation to existing communications with Belfast and its proximity to Lough Neagh (Fig. 8) it could be developed as a major industrial complex, specializing in electronic, mechanical, and scientific equipment, research, and development and the provision of recreational and leisure facilities. Alongside this, it was recommended that seven small towns in the Belfast region should be expanded and developed as 'Centres of Development' to accommodate a further 36 000 residents (Fig. 6, p. 35).

It was also suggested that steps should be taken to preserve valuable rural areas in the Belfast region for agriculture, forestry, and outdoor recreation. This, it was proposed, could best be done by public ownership of the most valuable and threatened areas, the preservation of rights of way, and the provision of access.

The Matthew report was generally accepted and put into operation by the Northern Ireland Government, though not without some amendments and one serious omission. A development 'stopline' was imposed on the Belfast area and though it came under severe pressure at times, it was quite successfully maintained. Unfortunately, however, the movement of population from the Belfast area to the regional centre and the expanded towns has not been on the necessary scale. Partly this is due to householders' reluctance to leave well-known districts when family and friends live close by. Partly it is because accommodation in the expanding areas is much more expensive than they have been accustomed to and they lack the necessary economic resources. To a large extent, however, it has been due to the fact that no arrangements

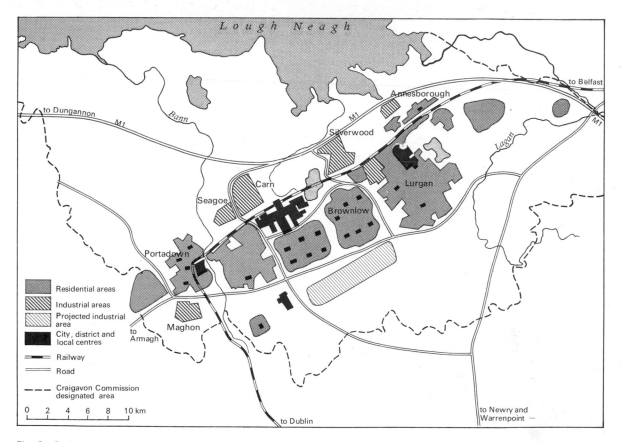

Fig. 8. Craigavon inner area plan

for large-scale movement of overspill population had been made. The result was that by the end of the 1960s the population of the Belfast area had already attained that 600 000 intended as the target for 1981. Two main proposals were made to deal with the situation. In 1969 the consultants on the Northern Ireland Development Plan suggested that the 'stopline' be extended to incorporate an additional 4200 hectares and thereby provide building sites to accommodate the population growth. It was also suggested that population mobility should be increased by the provision of loans and grants to cover disturbance and travel expenses and that the regional centre be given a higher priority by the Government.

In terms of its ability to attract new industry, however, the new centre of Craigavon had proved quite successful. The Goodyear Tyre Company set up a factory there which by the early 1970s was employing 1600 workers, and a Courtaulds subsidiary had also begun operations. Other towns originally suggested for expansion were also beginning to make progress by the early

1970s. In general they were up to the schedule for population expansion, industrial development, and house construction suggested in the original regional plan. Indeed, Carrickfergus, Ballymena, and Antrim in particular made notable progress. Branches of I.C.I., Courtaulds, and Carreras have been established at Carrickfergus, Michelin at Ballymena, and at Antrim British Enkalon expanded operations several times to the point where the original target population for 1981 was revised upwards. The delimitation and generally successful defence of the development 'stopline' ensured the survival of many of the rural areas in the Belfast region. Their preservation and use for recreation were carried out under the Amenity Lands Act (N.I.) of 1965. Under this legislation 7 Areas of Outstanding Natural Beauty, 27 Areas of Scientific Interest, and 12 Nature Reserves were designated for purposes of leisure, conservation, teaching, or research. Considerable efforts were made to reconcile scenic value with provision of facilities such as rights of way, access routes, planned walks, and refreshment centres. Finally, the New and Expanding Towns Act (N.I.) of 1965 provided for the creation of New Towns and the expansion of existing centres under a New Towns Commission vested with all normal municipal functions. It was used to aid the development of Craigavon (1965), Londonderry (1969), and the Antrim/Ballymena complex (1970).

The lack of continuous surveys of the urban areas remarked by Matthew in his report has since been remedied. In the late 1960s and early 1970s a series of Area Plans were prepared which outlined the proposed economic and physical development and interrelationships of specified rural and urban areas. The greatest task of all, however, concerned plans for the redevelopment of the Belfast Urban Area. These were prepared in two stages. The first, published in 1969 by a firm of town planning consultants, was largely concerned with physical and economic renewal and development. It endorsed the general policy of demagnetizing Belfast by restricting growth of population and housing and by concentration on Craigavon and the growth centres. It also suggested that this process should be expedited by the location of as many new government offices as possible in the growth centres, the establishment of overspill targets and phased overspill agreements between the local authorities of the Urban Area and the centres concerned, and the setting up of a Housing Coordinating Agency with differential housing subsidies to encourage house building in these centres.

On Belfast itself the report suggested that the housing redevelopment programme should be accelerated, standards of density and open space established, comprehensive improvement areas should be defined, and compulsory powers and incentives made available to ensure improvement. It was also recommended that the regional shopping function of the city centre should be retained and consolidated and twelve district centres established. Concentration of future industrial, office, and warehouse development in specific areas was also suggested, as well as integrated neighbourhood and district centres for social, educational, and recreational facilities. A separate Belfast Transportation Plan was issued by a second firm of consultants in 1970. Here the chief recommendations were an ambitious road plan, incorporating an urban motorway scheme, intermediate and centre ring roads, radial motorways, new regulations covering traffic flow and parking in the central area, and a new bridge over the Lagan. The Northern Ireland Government accepted these plans and work on their recommendations had begun by 1970 (Fig. 7).

Unfortunately, no serious efforts were made to solve the problems of residential segregation. The Urban Area Plan did involve the clearance of some small working-class areas noted for their sectarian militancy, but this was a by-product rather than a conscious intention. Indeed, there are factors at work which encourage perpetuation and reinforcement of the segregation. One of these mentioned earlier is the unfortunate fact that 'mixed' areas tend to be the flashpoints for incidents and riots in times of community tension and therefore segregation may be the best way to avoid such events and maintain the fragile civic peace. In view of this, past public authority decisions to allocate new estates to residents of one outlook alone are comprehensible. However, they may also have been influenced by considerations of local electoral geography. An area which is solidly Protestant or Catholic has a predictable political outlook, but unless the precise proportions of the two communities are known, 'mixed' districts are an uncertain factor. Consequently, the practice of allocating houses to households of one particular outlook was a useful way of confirming and consolidating existing voting patterns. Thus when Belfast Corporation assigned Ballymurphy estate in south-western Belfast to Catholics, this reinforced the overwhelmingly anti-Partition vote in that area at local Stormont and Westminster elections and left undisturbed the equally strong Unionist majorities in neighbouring seats.

5 The Future

Perhaps the ultimate tragedy surrounding the problems of Northern Ireland lies in the fact that after fifty years of experiment with a regional parliament, there were definite signs of economic and political progress which have now been jeopardized by an escalating series of political crises. On the economic front, despite the persistently high levels of relative deprivation in the form of unemployment, low incomes, and emigration, there is little doubt that progress had been made towards replacing the jobs lost through contraction of traditional industries, attracting high wage 'growth' industries and generally rationalizing and diversifying the economic structure. In political affairs there were signs in the mid-1960s that a decided thaw was under way, as evidenced by efforts to improve relations between Protestant and Catholic, meetings between the Premiers of Northern Ireland and the Irish Republic, and the installation of an Official Opposition. Progress in regional development was rather slower, particularly in recognition and prescription for the problems of the western areas, but the Matthew Report for the Belfast region had been produced and accepted and was being put into operation. Gradually the problems of the remoter areas also received recognition and in the designation of 'growth centres' the planners had probably reached an acceptable compromise between total neglect and purely social measures alone.

Unfortunately political developments after 1968 endangered all of these promising trends. Any slender basis of cooperation and understanding which was growing up was probably seriously damaged and opinion may have been polarized once again, thus confirming each of the communities in their respective nationalistic outlooks and their perception of each other. The actual physical damage inflicted on economic performance has been surprisingly small. Most of the destruction has been confined to wholesale and retail outlets in the central areas of Londonderry and Belfast. Many of these have reopened within a short time. Moreover, considerable British Government aid has been advanced to repair such damage and also to strengthen the shipbuilding and aircraft industries particularly. The real economic damage resulting from the political crises has been in the related fields of confidence and investment. Clearly the endemic communal violence and continuing military action are symptoms of a deep-seated political instability which discourages an inflow of risk capital. In addition, the very nature of the dispute in Northern Ireland deters investment. So long as the constitutional relationship of the province *vis à vis* Great Britain and the Irish Republic remains in doubt then potential investors will be dubious about economic prospects. It is hardly surprising therefore that there was practically no private investment in Northern Ireland during the three years following 1970, that bankruptcies reached a record level in 1971, and that some firms cancelled plans to initiate or expand industrial concerns there. The doubt surrounding the constitutional position applies particularly to the western and southern parts of the Province since there have been several suggestions that these areas should be ceded to the Irish Republic. Consequently, so long as an unfavourable 'image' and doubts about the constitutional integrity of Northern Ireland persist, then much-needed investment funds will not be forthcoming. In the short term this may not be too serious in view of the considerable financial commitment of the British Government, especially since March 1972. However, even this source of funds is not inexhaustible. It is merely being utilized as a stop-gap in an emergency situation and is no substitute in the long run for private investment. Indeed, if the absence of such investment continued over a long period then even the British Government's measures would not be sufficient to stave off serious economic difficulties. While it is true that in many ways the Northern Ireland economy is basically sound, exhibits considerable growth potential and has suffered surprisingly little direct damage, a long period of little or no new investment and very few new undertakings arriving from abroad could eventually cripple further development. Without these, a slow-down in growth, stagnation or possibly even contraction in employment opportunities are all possible. In such circumstances the progress and potential of the past years and the ambitious schemes for provincial and local development will become irrelevant.

Thus it would appear that settlement of the political problem is a pressing priority. This requires action on two fronts. On the military front it necessitated an end of I.R.A. activity, either by negotiation or by military effort. Both these courses were explored in 1972. On the purely political front it required the total restructuring of the institutions of government and administration in Northern Ireland. The eventual aim was to create a structure wherein the rights and privileges of both communities were guaranteed, policy formulation and decision-making were shared, and security was fairly administered in all areas. A conference of several of Northern Ireland's political parties was held at Darlington in September 1972 to discuss these ideas and a 'Green Paper' entitled 'The Future of Northern Ireland' appeared in November. Here the most significant item was probably the declaration that any settlement must be acceptable as far as possible, not only to both groups in Northern Ireland and to the British Government but also to the Irish Republic. Herein lies the crux of the political problem in Northern Ireland: in that any solution which does not propose further partition of the country or an exchange of population must face the task of trying to reconcile two conflicting sets of national loyalties within a single political area. The British Government's approach was to suggest the system of power sharing in an assembly elected by proportional representation. In other parts of the world similar problems have been tackled by such devices as written guarantees of citizens' rights, careful allocation and rotation of public offices, or varying degrees of federalism. However, each of these solutions requires a basic common desire for inter-community compromise and cooperation to make them function smoothly. It remains to be seen if such a desire exists in Northern Ireland, and how it could be expressed through suitable institutions.

In June 1973 elections were held under a proportional representation system for a new 78-seat Assembly to govern Northern Ireland

U.P.I

Further Work

There are several official sources of statistics on Northern Ireland. The most useful is probably the *Digest of Statistics* published in March and September each year. There is also the *Annual Report of the Government of Northern Ireland, Economic Section* and the *Ulster Year Book*, the official handbook of Northern Ireland.

The best recent histories of Ireland are:
BECKETT, J. C., *Short History of Ireland* (Hutchinson, London, 1952) and
—*The Making of Modern Ireland* (Faber, London, 1966).

The general geography of the country is considered in:
FREEMAN, T. W., *Ireland: A General and Regional Geography* (Methuen, 2nd edn. revised, 1960).
GILLMOR, D., *A Systematic Geography of Ireland*, (Gill and Macmillan, Dublin, 1971).
ORME, A. R., *Ireland*, No. 4 in 'The World's Landscapes' by J. M. Houston (ed.) (Longmans, London, 1970).

Aspects of the geography of Northern Ireland are dealt with by:
COMMON, R. (ed.), *Northern Ireland from the Air* (Queen's University, Belfast, 1964).
EVANS, E. E., 'The Personality of Ulster' *Transactions of the Institute of British Geographers*, **51** (1970), 1–20.
SYMONS, L., and HANNA, L., *Northern Ireland: A Geographical Introduction* (University of London, 1967).

The Economic Problem
Economic development in Northern Ireland is dealt with by a succession of consultants' reports and government publications. The most useful are:
ISLES, K., and CUTHBERT, N., *An Economic Survey of Northern Ireland* (H.M.S.O., Belfast, 1957).
Northern Ireland Development Programme 1970–5 (H.M.S.O., Belfast, 1970).
WILSON, T., *Economic Development in Northern Ireland* (H.M.S.O., Belfast, 1965).

Useful and comprehensive articles on recent economic changes are:

BUCHANAN, R. H., 'Five Year Plan for Ulster', *Geographical Magazine*, **42** (August 1970), 845–6.
STEED, G. P. F., and THOMAS, M. D., 'Regional Industrial Change: Northern Ireland', *Annals of the Association of American Geographers*, **61** (1971), 344–60.

Articles dealing with individual industries are:
STEED, G. P. F., 'Internal Organization, Firm Integration and Locational Change: the Northern Ireland Linen Complex, 1954–64', *Economic Geography*, **47** (July 1971), 371–83 and by the same author 'The Changing Milieu of a Firm: A Case Study of a Shipbuilding Concern', *Annals of the Association of American Geographers*, **58** (1968), 506–25.

Aspects of agriculture are covered in:
SYMONS, L. J., *et al.*, *Land Use in Northern Ireland* (University of London, 1963).

The Political Problem
Considerable care is necessary when reading any material on the political affairs of Northern Ireland. However, the following are useful:
BOAL, F. W., and BUCHANAN, R. H., 'Conflict in Northern Ireland', *Geographical Magazine*, **41** (February, 1969), 331–6.
BUSTEED, M. A., 'Northern Ireland: Geographical Aspects of a Crisis', *Research Paper*, No. 3, School of Geography, University of Oxford, 1972.
KEE, R., *The Green Flag: a History of Irish Nationalism* (Weidenfeld & Nicholson, London, 1972).
JACKSON, H., *The Two Irelands—A Dual Study of Inter-group Relations*, Minority Rights Group, Report No. 2 (London, 1971).
STEWART, A. T. Q., *The Ulster Crisis* (Faber, London, 1967).
'Sunday Times' Insight Team, *Ulster* (Penguin, London, 1972).
WALLACE, M., *Drums and Guns: Revolution in Ulster* (Geoffrey Chapman, London, 1970).

The best general geographical treatment of the Irish boundary question is:
HESLINGA, M., *The Irish Border as a Cultural Divide* (Van Gorcum, Amsterdam, 1962).

47

The work of the Boundary Commission and the curious story of its recommendations are in:

Report of the Irish Boundary Commission, 1925 (Irish University Press, Shannon, 1969), with an Introduction by G. Hand.

ANDREWS, J. H., 'The "Morning Post" Line', *Irish Geography*, **4** (1960), 99–106 and also 'The Papers of the Irish Boundary Commission', *Irish Geography*, **5** (1968), 477–81.

The history and development of Northern Ireland since partition are best covered in:

WALLACE, M., *Northern Ireland: Fifty Years of Self-Government* (David and Charles, 1971).

WILSON, T. (ed.), *Ulster under Home Rule* (O.U.P., London, 1955).

The structure and workings of the constitutional arrangements are discussed in:

LAWRENCE, R. J., *The Government of Northern Ireland: Public Finance and Public Services* (O.U.P., 1965).

MANSERGH, N., *The Government of Northern Ireland* (Allen & Unwin, London, 1936).

The curious nature of society and political life in Northern Ireland is covered by two splendid pieces of work:

BARRITT, D. P., and CARTER, C. F., *The Northern Ireland Problem: A Study in Group Relations* (O.U.P., London, 1962; 2nd edn., 1972).

ROSE, R., *Governing without Consensus: an Irish Perspective* (Faber, London, 1971).

Future prospects are discussed in:

KINGSTON, W., 'Northern Ireland, the Elements of a Solution', *Political Quarterly*, **43** (April–June 1972), 201–11.

The Future of Northern Ireland: A Paper for Discussion, Northern Ireland Office, H.M.S.O., London, 1972.

The Ulster Debate (Bodley Head, London, 1972).

Northern Ireland: Constitutional Proposals, Cmnd. 5259 (H.M.S.O., London, March 1973).

The Regional Problem

Aside from various sections in the 1970–5 Development Programme, little has been written on the economic problems of western Ulster. Two useful pieces of work are:

ROBINSON, A., 'Londonderry, Northern Ireland: A Border Study', *Scottish Geographical Magazine*, **86** (December 1970), 208–21.

Londonderry as a Location for New Industry Northern Ireland Economic Council, H.M.S.O., Belfast, 1966.

The political problems of this region have also been neglected, though several of the general works do contain reference to the practices of gerrymandering and discrimination. The regional divide in Protestant opinion is stressed in:

BOAL, F. W., and BUCHANAN, R. H., 'The 1969 Northern Ireland Election', *Irish Geography*, **6** (1969), 78–84.

Much more has been written on the political and economic problems of eastern Ulster and of the Belfast Region in particular. Useful sources on the growth and development of Belfast are:

BECKETT, J. C., and GLASSCOCK, R. E. (eds.), *Belfast: The Origin and Growth of an Industrial City* (B.B.C. Publications, London, 1967).

EVANS, E. E., and JONES, E., 'The Growth of Belfast', *Town Planning Review*, **26** (1955), 93–111.

Segregation and conflict in Belfast have received considerable attention. The most illuminating sources are:

BOAL, F. W., 'Territoriality on the Shankill–Falls Divide, Belfast'. *Irish Geography* **6** (1969), 30–50.

—'Social Space in the Belfast Built-up Area', in Stephens, N., and Glasscock, R. E., *Irish Geographical Studies in honour of E. Estyn Evans* (Queen's University, Belfast, 1971).

JONES, E., *Social Geography of Belfast* (O.U.P., London, 1960).

—'The Distribution and Segregation of Roman Catholics in Belfast', *Sociological Review*, **9** (1956), 167–89.

Careful and detailed accounts of the initiation, progress, and consequences of civic disturbances can be found in two reports:

Flight: A Report on Population Movement in Belfast during August 1971 Northern Ireland Community Relations Research Unit, Belfast, 1971.

Violence and Civil Disturbances in Northern Ireland in 1969 Tribunal of Inquiry, 1972.

Several aspects of the social and economic geography of Belfast are covered in work cited above, most notably Jones (1960) and Beckett and Glasscock (1967). Further useful sources are:

MATTHEW, SIR R., *Belfast Regional Survey and Plan, 1963* H.M.S.O., Belfast, 1963.

THOMAS, M. D., 'Manufacturing Industry in Belfast, Northern Ireland', *Annals of the Association of American Geographers*, **46** (1956), 175–96.